DISASTER
BLASTERS

DISASTER BLASTERS

A KID'S GUIDE TO BEING HOME ALONE

**KARIN KASDIN and
LAURA SZABO-COHEN**

AVON BOOKS ◆ NEW YORK

For each health or safety crisis described in this book, the authors discuss several courses of action but only **one** is recommended. Parents should read this book carefully with their children to ensure that the children understand the proper steps to take in case of a real crisis.

This book is meant to educate and prepare. It is not intended as a substitute for the advice of your physician or as an alternative to appropriate medical care. Despite every effort to offer expert and well-tested advice, it is not possible for this book to predict an individual's reactions to a particular first aid or safety measure. Neither the publisher nor the authors accept responsibility for any consequences that may result from the recommended health or safety measures prescribed in this book.

DISASTER BLASTERS is an original publication of Avon Books. This work has never before appeared in book form.

AVON BOOKS
A division of
The Hearst Corporation
1350 Avenue of the Americas
New York, New York 10019

Copyright © 1996 by Karin Kasdin and Laura Szabo-Cohen
Illustrations by David Redl and Mona Mark
Published by arrangement with the authors
Library of Congress Catalog Card Number: 94-34455
ISBN: 0-380-77723-1

Library of Congress Cataloging in Publication Data:
Kasdin, Karin.
    Disaster blasters: a kid's guide to being home alone/Karin Kasdin and Laura Szabo-Cohen.
    p. cm.
1. Latchkey children—Life skills guides—Juvenile literature. 2. Safety education—Juvenile literature. 3. Emergency management—Juvenile literature. [1. Latchkey children. 2. Children of working parents. 3. Life skills. 4. Safety.]
I. Szabo-Cohen, Laura.   II. Title.
HQ777.65.K37 1995 94-34455 613.6—dc20 CIP AC

First Avon Books Trade Printing: May 1996

AVON TRADEMARK REG. U.S. PAT. OFF. AND IN OTHER COUNTRIES, MARCA REGISTRA-DA, HECHO EN U.S.A.

Printed in the U.S.A.

OPM   10 9 8 7 6 5 4 3 2 1

In memory of
EMILY RACHEL SACHS
1976–1995
from her loving teacher Karin
and adoring cousin Laura
that even one child
stay safe and whole in Emmy's name

Acknowledgments

I send my deepest love and gratitude to my three sons: Daniel, who keeps me "cool"; Andrew, who keeps me laughing; and Zack, who keeps me young. And to my dearest husband, Harold, who loves me even when I am none of the above.

—KARIN KASDIN

For blasting my worst disaster, my thanks to Audrey Carvajal and Paule (Penny) Prebus. With great delight I acknowledge the contribution of my children: Benjamin—First Fan and constant encouragement; Fanya—my youngest and gentlest editor; and Micah—the one who gets me to actually work. And eternal gratitude to James, husband-of-husbands, Old World or New Age.

—LAURA SZABO-COHEN

Table of Contents

· ·

Foreword for Adults

....

How about a strong dose of the truth? The truth is, nothing we can write will assuage the guilt of parents who work outside the home as, every weekday at about 3:00 p.m., their children return to houses and apartments where the only thing awaiting them is a pre-prepared snack. The truth is, according to the Child Welfare League of America, 42 percent of American children between the ages of five and nine are home with no adult supervision either often or occasionally. For older children the figure reaches a staggering 77 percent. Up to 10 million children are alone most afternoons virtually every weekday. The truth is, anything can and does happen to these kids.

Neither as authors nor as mothers do we condone leaving young children alone. But reality must be addressed. Putting our heads in the sand will not equip the 10 million home-alone children with the life-skills formerly required only by adults—adults lucky enough to have learned these skills gradually and naturally with age and *supervised* experience.

The truth is, even the parent who works at home needs to leave intermittently for business, social, medical, personal, and family purposes.

HOW TO USE THIS BOOK

In order to, as we tell your kids, "de–borify" safety information, we interwove it with stories, plays, and monologues. Through these your children will meet six characters from three families, each family with different geographic, socioeconomic, ethnic, and situational profiles. What they have in common with each other and *your* children is a nineties sensibility, attitude, speech pattern…and exposure to danger.

We take these characters through a series of twenty-one challenges or mini-adventures organized as follows:

1. We bring each character to the brink of, or the middle of, a health or household crisis.
2. We present our readers with three possible strategies, then ask them to choose the one they believe will best avert catastrophe. These answers can be recorded on the tear-out score sheet.
3. We return to the scene and reveal what the characters chose to do.
4. We explain why the characters' choices were right or wrong.
5. We present a step-by-step explanation of the correct procedure.
6. We wrap up each challenge with a brief epilogue relating what later happens to the characters as a consequence of their actions.

The information we present is gleaned from *The American Red Cross First-Aid Handbook,* our local Red Cross chapter, police station, Poison Control center, fire department, and telephone company, and assorted pediatricians, school nurses, and psychologists. We include only the most widely recommended procedures and advice. However, we are well aware that due to the circumstances of individual households and the differing ages and abilities of children, your rules may veer from the norm. Thus we strongly encourage you to read the book with your child for two reasons: To educate *yourself* and to enable you to specify for your child when, how, and why your rules and guidelines diverge from ours. Example: The use of 911, which we consistently tell kids to dial when they're unable to cope independently or confidently with a crisis. While 911 is available throughout *most* of the country for obtaining emergency counseling and rescue, regions unserviced by 911 still exist. Emergency services and hotlines in these areas have separate phone numbers which residents must teach their families.

Parents (who up to now have had little if any choice of kid-friendly safety instruction), this book is for you as much as for your kids. Though we can't lower your guilt quotient, we can improve your children's ability to behave wisely and responsibly during your absences. And perhaps this can lower your terror quotient. Until national priorities, child-care options, and our workplaces catch up to your and our level of concern for *all* our precious children and those who must provide for them, this is the most our book can accomplish.

Foreword for Kids

Congratulations! By opening this book you have taken your first step toward becoming an astronaut.

KIDDING!

No really, by opening this book you have taken your first step toward becoming a...

DISASTER BLASTER!

WHAT? You say you're too cool for this?

WRONG!

Staying alive is cooler than being cool.

If we swear this book won't be boring, will you promise to read the next sentence?

This book is about safety.

Wait! You promised!

What would you say if we told you that the book you are now holding will make learning about personal and household safety skills...fun? Yeah, right. They told you that learning your multiplication tables would be fun too.

We're asking you to trust us for a chapter or two. That's enough to prove that we have de-borified this material. The characters you are going to meet didn't even want to be in this book, but now they're grateful we made them famous. And they're even more grateful they became Disaster Blasters.

A Disaster Blaster is any person who can handle frightening or complicated situations safely, independently, and most important, without panicking. In other words, sooner or later this book is for every kid.

HOW TO USE THIS BOOK

When you play a Nintendo game for the first time, or build a model, or play a board game, do you read the instructions first? Of course not! So we stuck the complicated instructions in the Foreword for Adults. Feel free to glance at it. This will make your parents feel secure.

Your Handy-Dandy Score Sheet appears at the back of this book. Tear it out and score it. Give yourself 5 points under OWNING THIS BOOK for owning this book. You will be needing this sheet as you proceed through these challenges, so try not to lose it. Give yourself 2 points under HAVEN'T LOST IT YET if you haven't lost it yet.

When you complete the book, you will add up your points and find out your Disaster Blaster ranking.

Introduction

(AND WE DO MEAN INTRODUCTION)

We would like to introduce you to the Lewis-Rochelles. Luc (pronounced Luke) is thirteen and a guitarist. Do you like his earring? Boys, would your parents let you get an earring like that? Give yourself 5 points under EARRING on the score sheet if they would. Girls, would your parents let you get a boy like that? Give yourself 5 points under EARRING if they would.

Izzy (short for Isobel) is eleven and a serious student. She was responsible and level-headed even before she read this book.

Chloe (pronounced Klo-ee) is five and emotionally fragile. That means she cries a lot.

The Lewis-Rochelles live in the North Dakota countryside in this charming house...except theirs is three-dimensional.

Ms. Lewis-Rochelle is an air traffic controller and her husband is a flight attendant. The Lewis-Rochelles both work full time. Luc gets home from school first and is there to receive his sisters when they arrive.

Every time the Lewis-Rochelle children almost destroy themselves or each other they do so in play form. You can act out their close-calls with your friends, siblings, or classmates. You will see this symbol whenever the Lewis-Rochelles appear.

Meet Stephanie Imoto. She is fifteen and on her way to receiving a national tennis ranking. Just look at her athletic body! Jealous? Us too. Her parents are divorced and Stephanie lives with her mother in a lovely apartment in a major metropolitan area. That means a big, sometimes dangerous city.

Ms. Imoto, Stephanie's mother, is a well-known architect, and because she often visits building sites, Stephanie can't always reach her easily even if she wanted to. Because Stephanie is an only child, her challenges are always presented in "first person" form. This means she is the only one talking, thinking, or writing, and she uses the word "I" a lot. When Stephanie is on the phone you will see:

When she is writing in her diary you will see:

On a tree-lined street in a quiet, suburban neighborhood live the Marshall brothers, Joaquim (pronounced Wah-keem) and David (pronounced Day-vidd). Joaquim is eleven years old. We told him to tuck in his shirt for this book, but he flatly refused. On the positive side, he is

responsible and protective of his little brother. Joaquim is very concerned about the health of our environment.

David is eight. He doesn't feel protected. He feels bossed around. He cheers himself up by doing such things as taking apart Joaquim's clock-radio and reassembling it as a toaster oven.

Ms. Marshall is a dental hygienist and Mr. Marshall is a commercial real estate broker. That means he sells office buildings.

David and Joaquim's stories are written in the form of…stories. They are symbolized by:

So now you've met your companions on the road to becoming Disaster Blasters. Please don't fight with them.

Now turn the page for your first challenge.

•••

Luc-ed Out:

What to Do if You're Locked Out of the House

This is Luc's housekey.

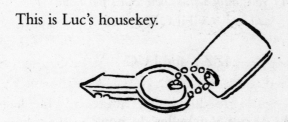

Too bad he threw it in the trash accidentally, along with his nutritious lunch, which he threw away on purpose. He is going to be in no mood to deal with being locked out of the house, especially when his two little sisters are due any minute. Where is he anyway? He's in a tree, trying to find an open window.

Uh-oh. It's starting to rain. We all know that during a thunderstorm being near a tree is one of the worst places to be.

Here come Izzy and Chloe up the driveway. Let's listen in.

IZZY

Luc, what are you doing up…Oh, no! We're locked out, aren't we?

1

CHLOE
(bursting into tears) *Waaaaaah!*

LUC
Oh great! Another hissy fit. It's a locked door, Chloe, not the ultimate tragedy of a busted Barbie head. All I have to do is break a window, climb in, and unlock the door.

IZZY
If you recall, Einstein, Mrs. Riley has an extra key.

LUC
No duh. Don't you think I tried her? She's not home.

CHLOE
Waaaaaah!

IZZY and LUC
Shut up.

What do the Lewis-Rochelles do now?
What would YOU do?

1. Go to a designated neighbor and ask to call a parent from there.
2. Throw a rock through a window and climb into the house.
3. Stop a car going by and ask for help.

   Mark your answer on the score sheet under **LUC-ED OUT,** and then come back.

Here's what the children did.

IZZY
This is ridiculous. I'm wet. The phone doesn't stop ringing. It's

probably Mom and Dad freaking out because we're not answering. Let's go to Mrs. Patel's house. Mom and Dad told us to go there when Mrs. Riley isn't home. (The three children go together to Mrs. Patel's.)

MRS. PATEL
Hi, kids. Hamid and Anjuli are at their grandmother's today. Why didn't you call instead of coming out in the pouring rain?

CHLOE
Luc lost our key and it's raining and Mom's at work and Izzy's hungry and Luc's angry and I'm crying!

LUC
May we please use your phone to call our mom?

MRS. PATEL
Of course, children. Come in. Shoes off. The phone's in the kitchen.

IZZY
(dialing) *Hello. This is Isobel Lewis-Rochelle. May I please speak to my mother? Hello, Mom?*

MOM'S VOICE
Izzy, I've been calling and calling.

IZZY
Mom, we're not home. We're at Mrs. Patel's. Einstein lost the key and we're locked out!

MOM'S VOICE
(slowly) *Oh dear. Well, you did the right thing, sweetheart. I'll be there in twenty minutes.*

IZZY
Thanks, Mom. Now why were you calling?

MOM'S VOICE
It doesn't matter anymore, lambchop.

Score yourself. If you chose **number 1, congratulations! You blasted that disaster!** Give yourself 5 points under **LUC-ED OUT.** By going to a designated neighbor (a neighbor your parents have selected as trustworthy) you avoided any possible danger. And by staying together you kept track of each other...you **remembered: There's safety in numbers.**

If you answered **number 2,** subtract 2 points. Unfortunately, many children think breaking a window and climbing through is the best and only way to get into a locked house. They are wrong. Broken glass causes far greater injuries than rain. **Remember: Inconvenience is always preferable to (better than) getting sliced to ribbons.**

We hope none of you chose **number 3,** but if you did, subtract 5 points. **Remember: Never, ever, for any reason get in a car with a stranger!**

As for the Lewis-Rochelles: The reason their mother was trying to reach them was to tell them they had just won a free trip to Disney World! They had three minutes to retrieve the winning ticket from Dad's dresser drawer. Needless to say, they lost out on the trip.

This may seem harsh punishment for losing a key, but hey, welcome to real life!

....

Beyond Gross:

What to Do When the Toilet Backs Up

This section of the book is rated D. It contains material that is disgusting, dirty, and darn-you-have-to-know-it-anyway. Can you think of anything more repulsive than an overflowing toilet? Neither can Stephanie Imoto, who is on the phone this very moment. Isn't eavesdropping fun?

OHGODOHGODOHGODOHGODOHGOD!
Megan, you have to come over. I mean it! I'm gagging! I'm barfing! I'm passing out! You won't believe what just happened to me! I came home like I do every day, and rushed for the bathroom. The plumbing in this apartment was put in when stegosaurus roamed the earth. So I

flushed like I flush every day…and…wait a minute—the memory is too fresh—I'm starting to gag again. Okay. I'm all right now.

Remember that volcano project we did in third grade with baking soda and vinegar? Well, that's what happened to the toilet. It just kept overflowing and overflowing. What do you mean, what did I do? I'll tell you what I did.…

What did Stephanie do?
What would YOU do?

1. Scream, close the door, and leave it there.
2. Scream and call the building superintendent (the person in charge of taking care of your apartment building), or a plumber.
3. Scream, turn off the water valve, and clean up the mess.

Mark your answer on the score sheet under **BEYOND GROSS** and come back.

Here's what Stephanie did.

I'll tell you what I did. I screamed. I panicked, and I stood there in shock, watching this steady flow of muck inching its way over the threshold into the living room and onto my mother's Persian rug, the only thing she loves more than me. I finally pulled myself together enough to call the superintendent, who came up within five minutes and saved the day. So what am I so hysterical about? you say. I'll tell you what I'm so hysterical about. This is the very superintendent whom I've had an eternal crush on since we moved here when I was seven. I've always believed if he could just know me on the inside he would fall in love with me. Well, he sure knows me on the inside now. Oh Megan, just let me die.

Score yourself. If you chose **number 3, congratulations! You blasted that disaster!** Give yourself 5 points under **BEYOND GROSS.** You've already learned that the little wedge-shaped handle on one side of the base of your toilet is a water valve.

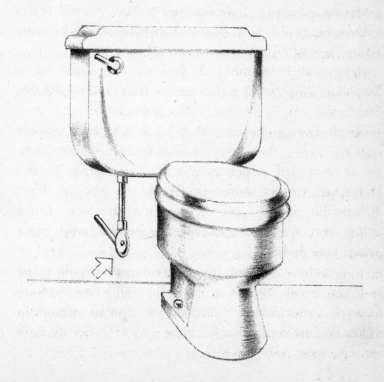

By turning it, you can stop the flow of water immediately. But did you know that there is also a water main somewhere in your house or apartment that will turn off *all* the water?

It's a good idea to have a grownup show you where this valve is, because all sorts of plumbing disasters can be blasted by turning off the water in your home.

If you chose **number 2,** you run the same risk as Stephanie. Subtract 3 points under **BEYOND GROSS.** Stephanie was lucky that embarrassment was her only problem. Even someone whose job it is to help you can end up hurting your body or your feelings. A dirty bathroom or ruined carpet, even if it's Mom's favorite, is a thousand times more preferable to being hurt. **Remember: Never, ever let anyone into your home when you are alone, except the people who come when you dial 911!**

If you chose **number 1,** you do not get any points. This is a very small disaster which you could have handled yourself if your parents had taught you how to turn off the water. Withhold affection for three days or until they show you the water valves.

As for cleanup, you know all those TV commercials you memorize? Bring one to mind that matches something in your cleaning supply cabinet, **read the directions carefully,** and use it, along with a lot of paper towels. Rubber gloves are hygiene-smart and handy for this type of cleanup. But remember to throw both gloves and paper towels into the garbage, **not** into the toilet, or you will cause a worse clog. If you are mature enough to stay home by yourself, you are mature enough to clean up by yourself. It is the considerate thing to do.

As for Stephanie, it so happened that the superintendent was also her designated neighbor, so her mother did not punish her for risking her safety. But Stephanie might as well have been grounded anyway, because it took her a solid week to clean the stains from the Persian rug.

···

Con-fuse-ion:

What to Do When the Lights Go Out

It was a dark and rainy night. Mr. and Mrs. Marshall were at Open School Night. The teacher began by telling the parents how David Marshall had secretly connected his tape recorder to the P.A. (public announcement) system, causing an hourly, school-wide concert of the Smashing Pumpkins.

David and Joaquim were at home being excellent by not killing each other. Joaquim was writing a letter on the computer to a buddy of his from Camp Wanageddawaya, complaining that the camp director had forced Sarah Scheinbaum to wear a shirt with her mermaid costume during talent night. What mermaid wears a shirt?

David was in his usual and favorite spot, his father's workshop, up to his elbows in batteries, wires, sharp tools, and no good. He knew he wasn't supposed to be here when Dad wasn't with him, but when Dad *was* with him, David never got to touch anything cool. Tonight, however, he felt he could do no wrong. After all, he was doing Dad a mega-favor by fixing the VCR. If he, an eight-year-old, could fix the machine his mother had been begging

10

his father to repair for the last month, surely there would be a big reward. If he could just get this itty-bitty gadget to connect to the black wire over...

"OH NO! WHO TURNED OUT THE LIGHTS? David, you little butthead. It's pitch black up here and I know it's your fault! Come here so I can kill you!"

"I'm coming up," David called, almost tripping over the flashlight on the basement stairs.

"Bring the flashlight," Joaquim yelled.

"I can't find it, it's dark down here," replied David. Once the boys met in the kitchen and Joaquim determined that his brother was okay, they attempted to plan a strategy together.

"Okay, David. There's no light. There's no heat. There's no hot water, there are no parents here, and worst of all, there's no TV! Happy, Copernicus? Dad is going to nail your ears to the wall."

"No, he won't." David smiled. "The VCR's almost fixed!"

What did Joaquim and David do?

What would YOU do?

1. Go out and get a flashlight from a neighbor.
2. Hunt together for a flashlight and use it to find the circuit breaker or fuse box and flip the correct switch(es).
3. Find Mom's candles and light them.

Mark your answer on the score sheet under **CON-FUSE-ION** and come back.

Here's what the Marshall boys did.

"David, where does Mom keep those fancy candles she uses when people who are not related to us come for dinner?"

"I used them for the stupid log cabin project I had to make for Social Studies. They're in my room. I'll get them."

"Okay. And we've got those great long fireplace matches. What color flame do you want?"

After lighting the candles, they each took one and sat on the rug singing camp songs.

Score yourself. If you chose **number 2, congratulations! You blasted that disaster!** Give yourself 5 points under **CON-FUSE-ION**. You shouldn't have to hunt for a flashlight, but if you do, go together. Every household should have several flashlights kept in a designated cabinet or drawer with other emergency items such as batteries, transistor radio, and fire extinguisher. These should be used *only* for emergencies. If you want to read under your covers get your own flashlight!

Houses can have one of two electrical systems. The first and most common is called a circuit breaker system. The other is a fuse system. Fuse systems are usually in older homes. Ask a parent which one your house or apartment uses. **If you use a fuse system, stay away from the main box. Playing with fuses can be dangerous!**

If you have a circuit breaker system use your flashlight to go find the circuit breaker box. Keep this book in a handy place and take it with you to help guide you through the next procedure.

What is a circuit breaker box? It is like a small cabinet with rows of switches inside. They look just like light switches. When everything is normal, these switches all point in the same direction. (They will all be pointing either to the left or right.) Sometimes you can "trip" a breaker by plugging in or using too many electrical items at once. When a breaker switch is tripped, it will no longer be pointing in the same direction as the rest of the switches. It will usually not be pointing right or left, but it will be right in the middle.

Most of the time you can fix the problem by flipping the switch all the way to the wrong direction first and then back to the correct position. The circuit breaker box is safe to use, so don't worry. It is usually located in a basement, garage, hallway, or closet. Have a parent show you where the circuit breaker box is in your house or apartment.

If all the circuits are tripped, there is often a main switch in the same row as all the other switches, and flipping it will also solve the problem.

If you flip one or several switches, and nothing happens, quit. Don't play around with the box. And make sure you have your parents' permission to use the circuit breaker box in the first place. Different parents have different rules about things like this. And the age of their child may make a big difference to them. They know you better than we do. You must follow the rules that have been set.

If you are not allowed to use the circuit breaker box, or if you flip switches and nothing happens, go to plan B.

PLAN B

Use your flashlight to call your parents, or another responsible grownup. If you are really in trouble, and don't have a flashlight, you should know by touch where the 0 for operator is on your phone. Call the operator and explain your situation. He or she will dial the number you need.

If you chose **number 1**, congratulate yourself for knowing you need a flashlight, but subtract 4 points for going outside alone in the dark. Are you enjoying the dark and the rain? Are you tripping on tree roots or sidewalk cracks? And who knows what danger lurks in the shadows?

If you chose **number 3**, subtract 5 points. **Remember: Never touch matches or light candles without a grownup by your side!**

The Marshall brothers could have been seriously burned if the candle had been too close to their hair or the living room rug or a nearby stack of newspapers. Let's not even mention the house burning down...that's a whole 'nother chapter.

As for David, was his father angry at him? You bet! David had indeed fixed the VCR, but big deal...he was forbidden to watch movies on it for a whole month.

Having a Ball:

What to Do if Someone Is Choking

A boring Thursday.

CHLOE

(rummaging through her goody bag in search of an after-school treat) *Where's my orange gumball? I saved it all week.* (She notices Izzy holding the gumball.) *That's my gumball from Juanita Susaret's birthday party! You can't have it!*

IZZY

Chill out piglet! The last thing you need is more sugar!

LUC

(picking out chords on his guitar) *Just give her the freaking gumball so I can hear my own music.*

IZZY

Music? Is that what that screeching is? Chloe, I've spent five years sharing my goody bags with you; you can spare one measly gumball.

CHLOE

Waaah!

IZZY

All right. You want it, greedy guts? Come and get it. (Izzy pops the gumball into her mouth and starts to run. Chloe takes up the chase. Izzy trips and starts to gag.)

CHLOE

Izzy, are you okay? Izzy? Answer me. Izzy! You can have the gumball. LUUUUUUC! Something's wrong with Izzy. (She runs to get Luc and unplugs his electric guitar.) *Luc, come fast! Something's wrong with Izzy!*

LUC

(not realizing that something is really wrong) *Yeah. It's called her personality.*

CHLOE

I'm not kidding! I don't think Izzy can breathe!

What does Luc do now?
What would YOU do?

1. Call a parent and ask for advice about what to do. Then do it.
2. Stick your finger down the victim's throat and try to remove the object she is choking on.
3. Have one person dial 911 while the other person per-

forms the Heimlich maneuver. If you are alone with the victim, perform the Heimlich maneuver first, then dial 911.

Mark your answer on the score sheet under **HAVING A BALL** and then come back.

Here's what Luc did.

LUC

(standing over Izzy) *Oh God, Izzy, can you talk? Can you breathe? You were right, Chloe. She's not faking. She's turning blue.*

CHLOE

It's my fault! Waaah!

LUC

Shut up, Chloe. Help me turn her over. Izzy, I'm gonna take care of this. Don't worry. (They turn her onto her stomach, and Luc pounds her on the back with his fists.) *Nothing's happening. Chloe, dial 911. Tell them our address first. Tell them our cross street is Route 443, and tell them your sister is choking and to hurry. I'm going to sit her up and stick my finger down her throat and try to get the gumball out.* (He sticks his finger down her throat, dislodges the gumball—which means he gets it unstuck—and Izzy coughs it up.) *Thank God. You're going to be okay, Isobel. We're going to get you a pillow and some water. And a blanket. And a towel. And call Mom. And call Dad. And wait until the rescue squad gets here.*

Score yourself. If you chose **number 3, congrat-**

ulations! You blasted that disaster! Give yourself 5 points under **HAVING A BALL.**

Here's how the Red Cross advises you to handle a choking disaster:

1. Always ask the victim if she can speak. If she can, her life is not in danger. It is impossible to speak without air. Coughing is also a good sign because coughing also requires air. If the victim cannot speak or cough, you must take care of this emergency immediately. Tell the victim calmly that you are going to help her.
2. Perform the Heimlich maneuver.

THE HEIMLICH MANEUVER
. . . .
FOR A CONSCIOUS (AWAKE) PERSON
OVER ONE YEAR OLD

Child, teenager, or grownup, **everyone** should know how to do the Heimlich maneuver. We are now going to explain how to do it. **This is no substitute for taking a certified CPR class.** CPR stands for Cardio (which means heart) Pulmonary (which means lungs) Resuscitation (which means to start again). So CPR is how you help someone who isn't breathing or whose heart has stopped. Why not take a CPR class with your whole family? Classes are offered throughout America by hospitals, schools, fire departments, rescue squads, and the Red Cross.

1. If the victim is not standing but is conscious, pull her up into a standing position.

2. Stand behind the victim.

3. Wrap your arms around the victim's waist.

4. Make a fist. Put the thumb side of your fist against the middle of the victim's abdomen (just above the belly-button).

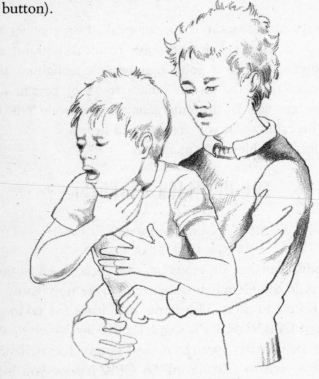

5. Grab your fist with your other hand.

6. Keep your elbows out like you are going to cluck like a chicken. Press your fist into the middle of the victim's abdomen and at the same time as you are pressing, push up. Don't be afraid to use force. Keep doing these press-pushes until the victim spits out whatever is choking her.

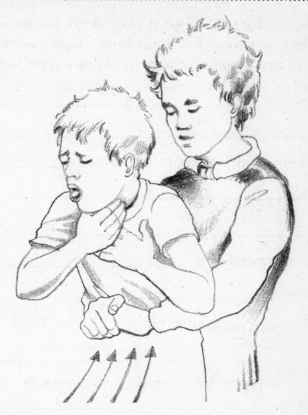

7. Help the victim stay calm and still, call 911, and wait together for help to arrive.

8. When the emergency squad arrives, you may take a minute to call a parent. When you explain to Mom and Dad what's happening, be calm because they may not be.

9. The emergency squad may or may not want to take the victim to the hospital. No matter what the decision is, be sure that the victim gets examined by a doctor as soon as possible.

Here's what you say when you call 911 and the order in which you say it. Fill in the blanks, make copies, and paste or tape a copy next to every phone in your home.

My address is _____

_____.

The nearest cross street to my house is _____

_____

_____.

My phone number is _____

My name is _____.

and I'm _____ years old.

I am _____.

(Tell whether you are alone, or with other people as well as the victim.)

Here's what I think is wrong with the person. Please come fast.

Stay on the phone. Someone will want to ask you questions. Answer clearly and calmly, and do what the person tells you to do. Don't hang up until you are told to do so.

If you chose **number 1**, sorry, subtract 5 points. We know it is natural to want to call your mom or dad in an emergency, but when someone is choking, you simply don't have the time. The rescue squad knows more than your parents about how to save lives. In a life or death situation, always call 911 before you call your parents.

If you chose **number 2**, Luc's choice, give yourself a pat on the back but zero points. You and Luc did the right thing by

- realizing how serious the situation was.
- calling 911.
- staying calm and comforting the victim.

The thing Luc did wrong was sticking his finger down Izzy's throat. It is very easy to push the object further down the throat or all the way into the lung. The Lewis-Rochelles were very lucky neither of these things happened. The truth is, Izzy did the stupidest thing of all. **Remember: Never ever run with anything in your mouth!**

If you are home alone, and worried about choking, it is a good idea to stay away from hot dogs, peanuts, and other round or sticky foods.

As for Izzy, she chews every mouthful of food fifty times before swallowing...while sitting very, very still.

As for Chloe, she felt very guilty for not sharing her gumball, so at dinner that evening she generously offered Izzy her broccoli.

Imperfect Strangers:

What to Do When a Stranger Comes to the Door

No, Alyssa, I'm not psychotic (crazy)...I do *so* have a good value system...I beg your pardon! Just because I want to attend this tennis clinic instead of going to the concert with you and half the school...Yes, I actually *am* weird enough to think Monica Seles is a bigger star than Jon Bon Jovi...

Hold on...there's the buzzer. I'll be right back.

It's the exterminator; he says he has a three-thirty appointment here. My mother didn't tell me she made an appointment, but we do have roaches with a bigger shoe size than I. I don't think I should let him in, but won't he charge for the housecall anyway?

What did Stephanie do?
What would YOU do?

1. Let the exterminator in to show him the dark, damp places where the roaches hang out.
2. Say to him, "You must be mistaken about a three-thirty

appointment. My mother never schedules appointments when I'm home alone."

3. Quickly making sure that your apartment door (or all the doors to your house) is (are) locked, tell him your parents are saying to please call and schedule another appointment. Now is not a good time.

Mark your answer on the score sheet under **IMPERFECT STRANGERS** and then come back.

Here's what Stephanie did.

Hi, Alyssa. Sorry it took two days to get back to you! I've been too upset to call anybody or even leave the house. No, don't worry. I'm fine. I didn't let that exterminator in, but if I had I could've been the girl in the newspaper. She did let him in and now she'll never be the same. Even when her wounds heal, how will she ever get this out of her mind? I feel like I should send flowers or something, but the newspaper didn't print her name. Do you think if I send them to the hospital they will know who they're for?

Score yourself. If you chose **number 3, congratulations! You blasted that disaster!** Give yourself 5 points under **IMPERFECT STRANGERS** for knowing **Never to open the door to strangers.** Your personal belongings, your physical and sexual safety, and your very life can be lost by a turn of the doorknob.

You also knew: **Never let a stranger know that you**

are alone. By pretending that you were getting instructions from your parents, you gave the intruder no clue that you were really alone.

If you live in an apartment, never buzz a stranger through the main door. You can help ensure the safety of all your neighbors by keeping strangers out on the street.

If you chose **number 1**, subtract 5 points. What happened to the girl in the newspaper happens to real kids every day in big cities *and* small towns. Losing five points is insignificant if you've learned a lesson.

If you chose **number 2, wrong, wrong, wrong! Subtract 5 points and remember: Never let anyone know that you are home alone!**

As for Stephanie, she was never able to think about her close call without feeling nervous or getting upset, but after a few days she was able to resume her normal life. As she told Alyssa, "The only good thing to come out of this is that other children may read or hear about what happened to that girl, and they won't have to learn their lesson the hard way."

This list is for a parent or guardian to fill in for and with you. If you don't lose it, you will always know exactly who to let into the house when you are home alone.

Family Members:

_____

_____

Neighbors:

_____

_____

Adult Friends:

_____

_____

Child Friends:

_____

_____

Repair, Delivery, and Postal Workers:

_____

_____

Salespeople:

_____

_____

Others:

_____

_____

Unfortunately there have been cases where criminals *dressed* like police or firefighters have been let into homes. **Let the police, firefighters, or rescue workers into your house only if you have called for them.**

Give the Guy a Break:

What to Do if Someone Breaks a Bone

The thousand-piece puzzle was waiting to be opened. Each of the Marshall brothers had a major report to complete by the next day. Plus, they were finally allowed to watch the repaired VCR and *Jurassic Park* had just been released on video. In other words, there was nothing to do.

Joaquim and David knew their house rule was no playing outside when their parents weren't home. But the school day was long, the bus ride was longer, and the twenty-seven Ho-Hos they ate didn't help to make the boys less restless. So they hung up their coats, brought their book bags to the den, turned on the television, laid out their homework…and began to wrestle.

You see, a serious crime had been committed: The corner of David's math book touched the tip of Joaquim's ruler. So of course Joaquim had to head-butt his brother in the stomach. David had no choice. He had to knee Joaquim where the sun does not shine. This sent Joaquim flying into the TV cart, which sent the TV flying onto Joaquim.

"You broke my ankle, you —!" Joaquim screeched.

David started to apologize but realized that his words couldn't be heard over Joaquim's sobbing. "What should I do? I don't know what to do," David cried.

Joaquim calmed down enough to say, "There's a television on my leg, genius. What do you think we should do? Help me...*ow*... get it off!"

Together David and Joaquim managed to jiggle and push the TV off the leg. Strangely, this seemed to make Joaquim's pain worse, and he lay back, breathing hard and unable to speak.

What did David do?
What would YOU do?

1. Ask the victim if he can move the ankle. If he doesn't answer, gently move his foot back and forth to see if he

has movement. If the foot moves, it's not an emergency and you can wait until your parents get home.

2. Help the victim to a comfortable bed or sofa, give him a drink of water, and dial 911.

3. Don't move the victim or touch the foot. Dial 911. While you are waiting for the rescue workers to come, call a parent or other caretaker, unless the people at 911 tell you to stay on the phone or keep the line free.

Mark your answer on the score sheet under **GIVE THE GUY A BREAK** and then come back.

Here's what David did.

David began to panic and Joaquim snorted. "It's not such a big deal, David. Just call Mom and Dad at work and get one of them to come home." And David did.

Score yourself. If you chose **number 3, congratulations! You blasted that disaster!** Give yourself 5 points under **GIVE THE GUY A BREAK**. Any possibility of a broken bone should be attended to by emergency medical workers. There are certain exceptions to this rule for adults, but there are no exceptions for children.

If you chose **number 1 or 2**, subtract 2 points. It's natural to ask a victim if he can move the body part that has been hurt. But this can cause further damage and more pain. Neither you nor the victim should move or touch the injury. Even if you think moving the victim might make him more comfortable, **never change the victim's**

position (except if he's in a life-threatening situation, like in a fire).

Swelling, turning black and blue, and pain are not the only signs of a broken bone. The victim may also have internal bleeding, respiratory (breathing) difficulties, or he may even go into shock. You are not experienced enough to deal with these problems. And that is why you must call 911 immediately, even if the victim says it's not so bad.

Please learn along with Joaquim that admitting you are in severe pain, allowing a younger sibling to be right, and being the center of a big, embarrassing scene are small prices to pay for being able to recover full use of your leg.

As for both boys, they finally learned why parents are always saying, "Keep your hands off each other. Someone's going to get hurt!" They remembered this lesson for a full two days.

Home on the Range:

What to Do If You Get Burned

Luc is in the family room with the TV on. He is also eating a big bowl of popcorn while he tunes his guitar and occasionally glances at his science notebook.

LUC

If I get anything lower than a C on this test I won't be allowed to get the iguana. Anyone who disturbs me for the next three hours gets scalped with my guitar pick.

CHLOE

But it's freezing outside and I want hot chocolate and you're the only one allowed to use the stove. (Izzy is sharpening her pencils, organizing her papers, and cleaning her glasses.)

IZZY

Make it for her, Luc. If I get an A on my extra-credit book report, Mom and Dad said I can get anything I want. I'm going to ask Luc not to get the iguana.

CHLOE

Lucky!

IZZY

If you could get an A by sheer luck, I wouldn't have to spend the next two hours in my room studying. (Izzy exits with her study aids.)

LUC

(going to the stove) *With or without marshmallows, oh great infantile, helpless, demanding one?*

CHLOE

With, of course.

LUC

Of course. (Luc boils the water and makes hot chocolate for Chloe. He turns the stove off and pours the hot chocolate into a mug.) *Now, scram!*

CHLOE

But I don't want this mug. I want my dinosaur mug!

LUC

The dinosaurs are extinct. And you will be too if you don't leave me alone. (He exits. Chloe pushes a chair to the stove to get her dinosaur mug which is kept in the cabinet above it. She checks to make sure the burner is not red, and then puts her hand on the burner to help pull herself up onto the stove.)

CHLOE

AAAAHHHH! AAAAHHHH! (Luc and Izzy come running. When they get to the kitchen, Chloe is lying on the floor clutching her hand. The chair has toppled.)

IZZY

Chloe, what is it? Oh my God! Luc, she's burned. Bad! What do we do?

What do the Lewis-Rochelles do now?
What would YOU do?

1. Put a generous amount of first-aid cream on your finger and rub it very gently over the victim's injury. Call a parent.
2. Immediately put the burn under cold running water or into a bowl of cold water. Wrap the burned area in clean, cold, wet towels, remembering to rewet the towels frequently. Call a parent.
3. Don't do anything, except dial 911.

Mark your answer on the score sheet under **HOME ON THE RANGE** and then come back.

Here's what the Lewis-Rochelles did.

IZZY

You'll be okay, Chloe. I'm going to put some ice on it.

LUC

No way! Ice will peel her skin off. Turn on the cold water. Chloe, can you stand up?

CHLOE

No.

LUC

Then I'm going to pick you up and sit you on the counter. You have to hold your hand under the cold water. Izzy, you stand next to her. I'm going to call Mom and Dad.

CHLOE

(still crying) *But it'll hurt!*

IZZY

But it'll help. (She helps Chloe put her hand under the water.) *Why did you touch the stove?*

CHLOE

It wasn't red so I thought it wasn't hot.

IZZY

Chloe, the burners stay hot for a long time after they aren't red anymore.

CHLOE

Well how was I supposed to know?

LUC

(entering) Dad's on his way. Let's get some clean towels and wet them.

CHLOE

Don't touch it!

LUC

We have to keep your hand cool so it'll stop hurting quicker. (He wraps her hand even though she is still crying, and as much as he hates doing it, he sings her "Dinosaurs on Parade." She stops crying.)

Score yourself. If you chose **number 2, congratulations! You blasted that disaster!** Give yourself 5 points under **HOME ON THE RANGE.** You and the Lewis-Rochelles did everything right. Cold water, whether from a faucet or a bowl, must be applied to burns immediately. If the burn is on a part of the body that can't be put under running water or into a bowl easily, skip that step and place cold, wet, clean towels directly on the injury. Remember to keep the towels wet and cold to absorb the heat from the burn quickly.

If you chose **number 1,** subtract 5 points. **Remember: The wrong ointment can interfere with proper healing!** Also, the germs you have on your hand will infect the victim when you touch her. Infections in a burn are serious.

If you chose **number 3,** don't add or subtract any points. This is one body-smart situation where you have an advantage over rescue workers because you are right there. Immediate treatment makes the rest of the healing process go much more quickly and safely. If you did call 911, don't feel bad. The people who answer the 911 calls are there so you never have to feel alone, and they are always patient and pleasant.

As for Mom, she moved all of Chloe's favorite dishes and snacks far away from the stove and onto a bottom shelf.

As for Luc, he failed his exam, but got the iguana anyway for his heroic handling of Chloe's burn.

As for Chloe, she can handle the bandage on her hand like a big girl, as long as she has her dinosaur mug and her dinosaur lunchbox and her dinosaur pillowcase and her dino…

You're Fired!:

What to Do if Something Catches Fire

Dear Diary,

Even you, who know every stupid thing I've ever done, won't believe this one. I, at fifteen and a half incredibly mature years, almost burned down myself and 820 of my closest neighbors. All in the name of stress reduction.

It was Sunday night. Monday after school was my chance to beat Penny Padoloupolis and win the regional tennis title. The only reason Penny beat me last time was because I was a little tense. Richie was there. Ever since that day in kindergarten when he glued his finger to his ear and I helped him tear it loose, he's had a crush on me. I knew he'd show up again, but I wasn't going to let it get to me.

I put on one of Mom's old records, any of which can put you to sleep in a nanosecond. I lit the incense candle that Alyssa gave me. And I must have been quite deeply relaxed because it was at least two minutes before I realized the pillow the candle was on and the bedspread were on fire.

What did Stephanie do?
What would YOU do?

1. Run for the fire extinguisher. If you don't know where it is, or you don't have one, **and the flame is still tiny,** use the non-burning part of the bedspread (or whatever else is handy) to smother the burning part. If you still can't put out the fire, run into the hall (if you live in an apartment), pull down the fire alarm, go to a designated neighbor's apartment to call 911, and leave the building immediately with that neighbor.
2. Grab your purse, your childhood teddy, your tennis racquet, and the photo album and leave the building. Call 911 from the corner deli.
3. Throw a pitcher of water on the fire. Refill the pitcher as needed.

Mark your answer on the score sheet under **YOU'RE FIRED** and then come back.

Here's what Stephanie did.

Oh Diary,

Thank heaven Mom's an architect. And thank heaven she's obsessed with safety. All I had to do was fly into the kitchen, grab the fire extinguisher, and zap the flames.

Whooaaa! I don't think they used that much foam in Ghostbusters. I not only annihilated the fire, I annihilated my pillow, my scrapbooks, my tennis racquet, threequarters of my wardrobe, and my dear, darling teddy.

Need I tell you that my experience with incense was not relaxing?

Score yourself. If you chose **number 1, congratulations! You blasted that disaster!** Give yourself 5 points under **YOU'RE FIRED.** All houses and apartments should be equipped with smoke alarms and handy fire extinguishers. The fire extinguisher won't be useful if it's located in the crawlspace under great-uncle Irv's old golf-clubs. It also won't be useful if you haven't learned how to use it. Make sure your parents or other caretakers show you how it works.

If the fire looks too big for you to handle, or if you don't know how to use a fire extinguisher, or if you have been instructed to leave your home no matter what size the fire is, leave your home immediately. If you live in an apartment, there should be fire alarms on every floor. Break the glass and pull the alarm. Then immediately get a designated neighbor to stay with you as you leave the building and wait for instructions from the fire department. If you live in a house, go immediately to a designated neighbor's home and call the fire department. Stay at your neighbor's house until you are instructed otherwise by a firefighter.

If you chose **number 2**, subtract 5 points. **Fire triples its size every minute. There is no time to grab belongings, even if they are special to you. Your life is your most precious possession.**

If you chose **number 3**, subtract 5 points. You couldn't make enough trips to the faucet for the water you would need to put out that fire. A pitcher of water will not permanently put out a fire larger than a candle flame. Smothering a small fire with a wet towel or blanket or coat or jacket or anything made of cloth is the best solution for someone who doesn't have a fire extinguisher handy.

As for Stephanie, during the regional championship

game she fell three times, dropped her borrowed racquet twice, and got four double faults. Not only were Richie and the entire crowd staring at her, but the game was on cable TV. The next time she wanted to relax she took a nap.

Duty and the Beast:

What to Do if an Animal Gets into the House

The last time Quarrystone Elementary School closed early was in 1963, the day President Kennedy was assassinated. It rarely snowed in Florida, and when it did the school system panicked...there was only one snowplow for all of Lower Dudley County.

David and Joaquim knew the family rule was to go right into the house after getting off the bus. But perhaps their parents made the rule only for when the bus arrived at the regular three-thirty time. Today they were off the bus at 11:00 a.m. The lawn, which only this morning had looked dead and brown, now looked like a huge cinnamon pancake sprinkled with sugar. They scooped as much snow as they could into their hands and managed to make a snowball the size of a Tic Tac.

Joaquim needed to go to the bathroom. "David, come with me."

"No way!"

"Yes way. You're not allowed to be outside alone and you know it. We'll be back out in four minutes."

"The snow could be melted by then!"

Joaquim pulled his brother inside by the beltloop. David bellowed, "Cut it out, Joaquim! You're giving me a wedgie!"

Just then they heard a scratching noise coming from the direction of the family room. David started to walk toward the sound, but Joaquim, who was still holding his brother's beltloop, pulled him back. "Are you crazy, David? It could be a burglar in there."

"Cool," David said in the way that Mom hated. He broke free and charged into the family room to see the fireplace screen knocked down, and a panic-stricken squirrel tearing apart the furniture in its desperation to get back outside.

"Cool," David repeated.

What did David and Joaquim do?
What would YOU do?

1. Offer the animal some lettuce leaves and some of Mom's expensive whole, jumbo, unsalted cashews. Turn him into a pet.
2. Open all the doors to the house and try to chase him out.
3. Leave the house. Go bother that designated neighbor who's getting pretty sick of you by now. Ask him or her to call your parent or an exterminator. Stay at the neighbor's house until the animal is removed.

Mark your answer on the score sheet under **DUTY AND THE BEAST** and then come back.

Here's what the Marshall boys did.

"Not cool," Joaquim responded as he advanced toward David. "I think we should get out of here."

"If you give me one more wedgie, I'm going to tell my squirrel to attack you!"

"*Your* squirrel?"

"Yeah, mine. And I'm going to turn him into a pet." David turned toward the squirrel, which by now was clawing at Dad's leather chair. "Are you hungry? I have acorns from my Pilgrim diorama."

The squirrel didn't answer. It stopped racing around, crouched down low staring at the boys, bared its sharp teeth, and gave out a terrified and terrifying screech. Suddenly it didn't seem like an animal that could become a pet.

Joaquim, trying very hard not to panic, said quietly, "David, come with me. Now." David and his big brother walked slowly but steadily out of the family room, closing the door behind them. They went across the street to Mrs. Levinson's house. She would know what to do.

Score yourself. If you chose **number 3, congratulations! You blasted that disaster!** Give yourself 5 points under **DUTY AND THE BEAST.** Review the answer. No explanation needed.

If you chose **number 1,** subtract 5 points. We hope you are not afraid of shots from very long needles. Wild animals are likely to have rabies. Rabies is a disease that humans can catch if bitten. It is fatal, which means you will die from it if you don't get treatment immediately. The treatment is a series of injections very different from the allergy, measles, or flu shots you may have had. If you do get bitten, remember the disease is far worse than the shots. Get help immediately.

Wild animals are not meant to be pets, no matter how furry and cute they look. Old TV reruns often feature stories about children who bring home wild animals and tame them. Of course, the animals you see on TV are not really wild at all. They are animal actors bred in captivity, and they are always under the watchful eye of special trainers.

If you chose **number 2,** subtract 3 points. You knew the animal needed to get out, but you didn't know that you are not the one to do it. Again, let a neighbor or your parents get the exterminator on the case. Even if your trustworthy neighbor gets sick of you, that neighbor was chosen by your parents to be someone who won't bite you for bothering him or her.

As for David and Joaquim, they were able to make even better snowballs from the stuffing that the squirrel tore out of the family room sofa.

As for Mom, unfortunately even a desperate squirrel couldn't destroy Dad's hideous but sturdy favorite chair.

....

Vitamin B-Careful:

What to Do if You Swallow Poison

A late afternoon in May. Luc and Izzy are working on a project at the kitchen table. Chloe approaches.

CHLOE

That's a funny-looking guitar. It's made of wood…and where's the plug?

LUC

This is not an electric guitar, ignorant short person. This is called an acoustic guitar. You don't plug it in.

IZZY

It's the kind they played when Mommy and Daddy were young…before electricity was invented. We're going to build one from scratch for my gifted class final project. Luc is helping me.

CHLOE

Can I help too?

IZZY

No, Chloe. The last time you pushed your face into our business, you ruined the cake we were decorating for Mom's birthday. It ended up saying "Happy Birthemdkyugndk." You are not big enough to help this time. (Chloe takes another step forward. Izzy and Luc brush her aside firmly.)

47

CHLOE

WAAAHHH! I hate you! You think you can beat up on me just 'cause you're bigger? I'll show both of you! I know how to get big fast! (While Izzy and Luc concentrate on their work, Chloe gets her vitamins out of the cabinet. She empties the whole bottle into her lap and chews up almost all of the tablets. Izzy goes to the cabinet for the glue and suddenly sees what her sister has done.)

IZZY

Oh my God, Chloe! What are you doing?

CHLOE

I'm getting bigger and stronger than you. I feel it happening already!

What do the Lewis-Rochelles do now?
What would YOU do?

1. Drink lots of liquids and wait to see if any symptoms develop.
2. Call Poison Control immediately and follow their instructions.
3. Have the victim stick her finger down her throat in order to make herself vomit up the poison.

Mark your answer on the score sheet under **VITAMIN B-CAREFUL** and then come back.

Here's what the Lewis-Rochelles did.

IZZY
Chloe, this is very important. You could get really sick from what you did. Tell me how many vitamins you ate.
CHLOE
I have to think. I had five Freds. I ate about twelve…no, about thirty Wilmas. I bet I had two hundred Pebbles. They're lavender!
IZZY
Chloe, I hate to tell you this…Luc has to stick his finger down your throat and make you throw up. Luc, I hate to tell you this, but…

LUC
I don't think so!

CHLOE
I can't believe that you guys are older than me, and you don't know that vitamins make you healthy, not sick.

LUC
Wrong! Even things you think are good for you, like vitamins and medicine, can hurt you if you take too much. I think a whole

bottle of vitamins with iron is too much. And I think Izzy's right. You have to puke. But I think we should check with Poison Control. (Luc gets the number of Poison Control from the list of emergency numbers above the kitchen telephone. He calls).

LUC

Hello. My sister ate a lot of vitamins with iron…I don't know how many, but a lot…she's five…about five minutes ago…no, I'm the oldest one here…thirteen. Syrup of what?…Izzy, write this down. I-P-E-C-A-C. Yeah, I think we do have that…Yeah, I know what a tablespoon is…Yes, we have a medicine measurer…No, I'm not scared…Okay. Thank you.

IZZY

(entering with the Syrup of Ipecac) *I found it in the medicine cabinet. How much does she need?*

LUC

Two tablespoons and give the lady some room. Let's give it to her in the bathroom. Near the toilet. No, on the toilet. You call Mom or Dad.

CHLOE

Luc, there is nothing in the world you can do to make me throw up. I hate throwing up. I won't throw up.

LUC

Oh no, Chloe. You're wrong. There are many creative things I can do to make you puke. But since I'm in a hurry I am simply going to hold your nose and shove the Ipecac down your throat. (Izzy returns from phoning her parents.) *Izzy, hold her down. But get a raincoat.*

CHLOE

Okay, I'll take it. Don't hold me down! (Chloe swallows two tablespoons of the Syrup of Ipecac and we will spare you the details of what happened next).

Score yourself. If you chose **number 2, congratulations! You blasted that disaster!** Give yourself 5 points under **VITAMIN B-CAREFUL.** Like Izzy, you knew that too many vitamins can be as dangerous as poison.

Like Luc, you knew that Poison Control must be called any time children are home alone and someone ingests (eats or swallows) something questionable.

Chloe didn't have to see a doctor because Poison Control did not feel this was an emergency. Also, by talking to Luc they could tell that he was responsible enough to do the right thing. Sometimes Poison Control advises children to call 911. Treatment is different almost every time, depending on the poison and the age and weight of the child. **Do whatever Poison Control tells you to do, and make sure their phone number is listed with your other emergency numbers above every phone.** Equally important is having the correct emergency care items in the house. See pages 116–117 for The Perfect Disaster Blaster Medicine Cabinet.

Syrup of Ipecac is a medicine that forces you to throw up. Everyone should have a bottle in a safe place out of the reach of young children.

If you chose **number 1,** subtract 5 points. Many people wrongly believe that water flushes poison out of the body or dilutes it enough not to be dangerous. Don't count on it. Water often does nothing to help a poison victim. Why wait to see what happens when one of the things that can happen is death?

If you chose **number 3,** subtract 3 points. In Chloe's case, throwing up was the correct thing to do. However, this is not always true. There are poisons that will burn you seriously coming back up your throat. This is why you must always ask for guidance.

As for Luc, Mr. and Ms. Lewis-Rochelle were so happy and relieved that he had done the right thing and that Chloe was okay, they forgot to scream in his face that he hadn't been watching Chloe carefully enough.

As for Chloe, instead of getting big and strong she now weighs four pounds less. And she always asks permission, even before eating an apple.

Hot Shot:

What to Do for Heat Illness

Maaaa! Would you calm down! I wouldn't even have called you if the stormtroopers here didn't insist on it…I'll tell you everything in a minute…but first give me the insurance information…the Emergency Room Lieutenant is here holding me hostage until I give him your insurance number.

Hillary Life and Casualty, Group Policy Number 94587694847394-3947509694734-A. Satisfied, sir? May I please speak to my mother in private now?

Ma, the ambulance ride was so cool…why are you screaming?…I want to tell you about the ambulan…It started happening on the court. If there'd been any shade there it would've been ninety degrees in it. Yes, I wore my sunscreen…I didn't get a sunburn, I got "heat exhaustion"…yeah, that's what they call heat prostration these days.

Yes Mother, I felt leg cramps. Yes Mother, I know they're a warning sign, but I never let little things like that slow me down. Nancy Kerrigan was on the ice three days after a hired assassin mangled her leg with a lead pipe. Of course I knew to keep drinking. But I left my Gatorade in my locker and I didn't feel like walking all the way back to the building for it. Anyway, this driver was so cute...Yes Mom, I would've gone to my locker after the match, but I was in a hurry to get home...Ma, didn't you hear me...I'm fiiiiine! Honest! How was I supposed to know the air conditioner in the apartment wasn't working? It was working when I left this morning. So when I got home I still had the leg cramps. I drank some Gatorade, which didn't seem to do a whole lot of good by that point, and I started feeling faint. I didn't panic because Coach Chang's been teaching me about heat exhaustion since I started with him when I was eight. I took my temperature—it was 102—and I checked my face in the mirror—it was bright red and coated with sweat—so *then* I panicked.

...Ma, the ambulance driver has been studying *architecture*! Isn't that a coincidence? In fact, he likes a lot of the same things you like...

What did Stephanie do?
What would YOU do?

1. Take a cold bath.
2. Dial 911.
3. Drink anything you can find in the house and take an aspirin to immediately lower the fever.

Mark your answer on the score sheet under **HOT SHOT** and come back.

Here's what Stephanie did.

...Why are you still yelling? I handled it. The apartment couldn't cool off and neither could I. I knew I shouldn't take a bath while I was alone and dizzy. So what choice did I have...I had to call 911. While I waited for the ambulance I wrapped myself in cool, wet sheets, but not the Bloomingdale's ones. And here I am...No, don't come! All you've talked about for a month is the importance of tonight's meeting. I won't be responsible for you losing your first European contract because I was too lazy to fetch my Gatorade. Coach Chang can take me home. Okay, stop ranting and pick me up yourself. Maybe that ambulance guy I gave your phone number to is still here...Oh, I didn't tell you that part yet? Mom, he can't wait to meet you...I guess about twenty-four ye...So what? I met the woman *Daddy's* dating. She looks like a teenager! Bye, Mom...Mom? *Mom?*

Score yourself. If you chose **number 2, congratulations, you blasted that disaster!** Give yourself 5 points under **HOT SHOT.** You and Stephanie knew you were nearing the point of no return. Heat exhaustion can turn into heatstroke, and heatstroke can sometimes be fatal. Here are the steps to take for cooling down.

- Drink beverages such as Gatorade. Gatorade and products like it contain electrolytes, which help prevent dehydration. These products are the best choice, but if you don't have them the next best drink is salted water. **Recipe: One teaspoon of salt. One quart (4 cups) of cool water. Mix. Drink $\frac{1}{2}$ of a cup every fifteen minutes.**

- Move into the shade, a cool room, or an air-conditioned building or car.
- Pour a bucket of water over yourself, **avoiding the face,** or spray yourself with a hose, **avoiding the face.** This step should **not** be taken if you are faint or confused.
- Wrap yourself in wet towels or sheets. Evaporation is a great cooler-offer.
- Place cold compresses on your neck, groin (crotch), and armpits. (Remember, as with all cold compresses, **no ice directly on the skin.**)
- Immerse yourself (cover yourself up to your neck) in cold water—a bath, lake, or stream—**if someone is with you!**

You can gradually stop these cooling measures when your temperature descends to 100 degrees. But keep taking your temperature every four hours: In cases of heat illness body temperature can rise and fall rapidly.

If you chose **number 1,** subtract 2 points. Taking a cold bath is the right thing to do only **if you are not alone.** You may immerse the victim in cold water when *you are the caretaker.* **Remember: Even if your parents allow you to bathe and shower when you are alone, never do so when you are dizzy, faint, or confused due to heat illness or anything else.**

If you chose **number 3,** subtract 5 points. Some liquids

can actually be harmful in cases of heat illness. Regular colas have caffeine, which stops the body from correctly controlling its own temperature. And don't substitute salt (sodium) tablets for that salted water! Even if your parents have these tablets on hand, this is not the time to use them. You need the sodium, **but only if it is dissolved in water**.

As for Stephanie, even when playing on an indoor court in January, she constantly drinks from her four Thermoses of Gatorade. Of course she hasn't been in any of the team pictures because she's always in the bathroom after the match.

As for Ms. Imoto, she ran to her daughter's side. And after making certain that Stephanie had recovered, she reluctantly agreed to meet Louie the Ambulance Driver. They are still dating.

Scraping By:

What to Do if You Scrape Your Skin

The Quarrystone School bus #65 was making its last trip before being sent to the Home for Retired Schoolbuses, but neither of the Marshall brothers noticed the bumps or squeaks or gas fumes. Each boy was deep in private thought, inventing ever newer strategies to be the first one to reach the Nintendo.

As #65 came to a shrieking halt, the Marshall boys were already illegally out of their seats and rudely climbing over bodies in order to be the first one off the bus. As they ran home, they could barely hear the bus driver threatening to send their parents another pink slip for Misbehavior On District Transportation.

Hope filled David's heart. His pulse quickened, nearing Pearl Jam intensity. It never occurred to David that his older brother's legs were a full eight inches longer than his own. Jumping over the neighbor's daffodil bed was a piece of cake since he was not weighed down by his new, huge, expensive Charlotte Hornets book bag. He landed beautifully...dead center on the patio...but with one small miscalculation: His knees hit the concrete before his feet did.

David cried out a word he was not allowed to say. "—! Joaquim, I'm bleeding to death!"

"I'll be there in a minute," Joaquim yelled back, "just as soon as I get off Level Four of Blood Mission Laser-Sisters."

What did David do?
What would YOU do?

1. Go inside to the bathroom. Wash your hands thoroughly with soap and water, and using a *clean* washcloth, do the same to your scrape. Scrub as hard as necessary to remove all dirt and pebbles. Apply antibiotic ointment with a clean finger and cover the scrape with a Band-Aid.

2. Do everything the same as in #1, except don't apply the

antibiotic with your finger, which might be germy. Do it with a cotton ball.

3. Don't be a coward. A scrape is nothing. Beat up your sibling and take over the Nintendo.

Mark your answer on the score sheet under **SCRAPING BY** and then come back.

Here's what David did.

David limped to the bathroom mumbling under his breath. "Joaquim got lucky today. The daffodil bed was a bad idea. But tomorrow I've got a foolproof plan: I'll get up in the middle of the night and remove all obstacles from between the back door and the bus stop! I'll put the garbage cans on Joaquim's favorite shortcut. And I'll give little Jimmy from next door a quarter to hold the door open for me at precisely 3:26 p.m." He took the bar of soap and washed his hands. He grabbed a washcloth from the linen closet and soaped it up, using it to gently but thoroughly clean his knee. He squeezed some antibiotic cream on his finger and applied it to the entire scrape. Then he put a sterile gauze pad on top, securing it with waterproof first-aid tape. "Or I could just run faster."

Score yourself. If you answered **number 1, congratulations! You blasted that disaster!** Give yourself 5 points under **SCRAPING BY**. You and David did everything right.

If you answered **number 2**…Psych! Subtract 2 points

for letting us trick you into thinking you knew it all. Even though cotton or a Q-tip seems like it would be more sanitary and thus safer than your finger, the fuzzy fibers can become embedded (stuck in) your wound! And after all, you *have* washed your hands.

If you answered **number 3**, subtract 5 points. A scrape is only nothing if you know how to treat it. Without proper treatment even the smallest injury can become infected, and even the smallest infection can become something worse.

As for David (who is not a stupid boy), he finally realized that Joaquim's legs would be longer than his for at least another five years. So he made a secret deal with Sarah Scheinbaum. He promised to fix her Walkman, her electric curling iron, her hot rollers, her bike, and whatever else she might break over the next eight months. In return Sarah agreed to phone Joaquim at exactly 4:03 every day after school.

As for David's state-of-the-art Charlotte Hornets book bag, it had not weighed him down because in his rush for the Nintendo, he had left it on the bus. It now resides at the Home For Retired Schoolbuses.

Cool, Dude!

What to Do in Case of Mild Frostbite

A freezing cold day in February. The snow is two feet deep. It would be higher than Chloe's boots, if she had remembered to bring them home from school. Luc is already throwing snowballs at his sisters as they step off the bus.

LUC

BULL'S-EYE! Izzy Lewis-Rochelle blitzed and taken out! Will she rise again? Yes! Time for the White Cannon to take his perfect aim once more...

IZZY

Don't even think about it. Are you never going to grow up?

CHLOE

Yeah! I'm telling Mommy and Daddy that you aren't waiting for us in the house. And I'm telling them that you climbed the too-high tree. And I'm telling them that you threw a snowball right in Izzy's face when you're not allowed to. And I'm telling...(She is cut short when Luc throws a snowball at her mouth.)

LUC

There. Now you have something else to tell them!

CHLOE

I bet you think I'm going to cry, don't you? Well, I'm not! (She makes a snowball and throws it at Luc. It misses, of course. Luc climbs down from the tree, and a snowball war ensues (follows). After a half hour, the children trudge into the house and remove their coats, hats, and boots. Chloe goes into the kitchen to look for her snack.)

IZZY

Get back here, Chloe. You have to leave your boots in the laundry room!

CHLOE

I already left them at school!

IZZY

You're kidding! You've been out all this time without boots? Aren't your feet cold? Don't they hurt?

CHLOE

How did you know?

IZZY

Are you crazy? Don't you know you could get frostbite? Why didn't you say something?

CHLOE

I'm practicing being a big girl. Can we have ice cream for snack?

LUC

No offense, Chloe, but I do not see a career as a nutritionist in your future. Dare I suggest something warm might be called for on a twenty-seven-degree day? Windchill factor not included. (Chloe follows Luc into the kitchen. He notices that she is walking funny.) *Why are you walking like that?*

CHLOE

Like what? (Luc and Izzy hurry to remove Chloe's wet sneakers and socks.)

IZZY

Oh my God! Your feet are so red!

CHLOE

If they didn't hurt so much, they'd be just like the ruby slippers in The Wizard of Oz.

What do the children do now?
What would YOU do?

1. Wrap the frostbitten area in a heating pad. If you have no heating pad, aim a blow dryer at the area.
2. Massage the frostbitten area.
3. Rewarm the frostbitten area by immersing it in warm, not hot, water. Call for help.

Mark your answer on the score sheet under **COOL, DUDE!** and then come back.

Here's what the Lewis-Rochelles did.

LUC

I know what to do. Tamara Vishnesky Rollerblades to school no matter what the weather is. Her face got frostbitten once. The school made a big-deal life lesson out of it for the entire seventh grade. We have to put her feet into warm water.

IZZY

Check. (Izzy fills a plastic tub with water, checking to see that the water is comfortable against her skin, and instructs Chloe to sit on a chair and soak her feet. Chloe does. Several minutes pass.)

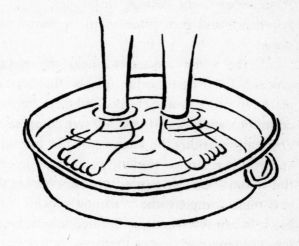

CHLOE

WAAHHH! (She takes her feet out of the water.)

LUC

Keep them in, Chloe! I know it really hurts when your feet start coming back to life, but not as much as amputation.

CHLOE

What's amputation?

LUC

Never mind. Izzy, call Mrs. Patel.

Score yourself. If you chose **number 3, congratulations! You blasted that disaster!** Give yourself 5 points under **COOL, DUDE.** Like Luc, you knew the proper way to begin frostbite treatment.

REWARMING MILD FROSTBITE

- Make sure the victim is warm and dry.
- Remove any tight clothing or jewelry.
- For hands and feet, place them in warm *(not hot)* water.
- Swish the water around to help the rewarming process. To rewarm other places that cannot be placed in water (noses, cheeks, and faces are the most common), apply warm *(not hot)* wet compresses.
- During rewarming the victim may feel burning pain and you may notice swelling or changes in color of the victim's skin. No matter what discomfort occurs, you must complete the warming process. You will know when rewarming is finished when the skin is soft and sensation (feeling) returns.
- Call whichever adult can reach you the most quickly. The next step is to apply a sterile, dry dressing (bandage) to the affected area, and an adult must do this.

If you chose either **number 1 or 2,** subtract 5 points. Direct heat (number 1) or touching the frostbitten area (number 2) can result in nerve damage or God forbid, amputation.

HOW TO TELL WHETHER FROSTBITE IS MILD OR SERIOUS

Mild Frostbite: **The only frostbite disaster you may learn to blast**
- skin that is red and painful

Medium Frostbite: **CALL 911**
- skin that is white and numb because tissue is frozen

Severe Frostbite: **CALL 911**
- blisters
- black skin (gangrene)
- hard, frozen skin

As for Chloe, she never left her boots in school again. She did leave her nineteen-foot-long pink paperclip chain, two fake diamond clip-on earrings, her Little Cupcake stick 'em memo pad, and her football.

Bee-ware:

What to Do When You're Stung by a Bee

It was Mother's Day and David knew exactly how he was going to surprise Mom. She wanted a new coffeemaker. Hers ground the beans, measured the amount of coffee and water, prepared it while you slept, and told the time (here and in four other time zones). The only thing it didn't do was keep the coffee hot. This was the twelfth coffee pot Mom had bought in three years. All of them made superb cold coffee. But David could fix anything.

Not only did he beef up the heating element, the clock could now tell the time in Jamaica. And this was the part Mom would really love: David had painted bright orange roses on the coffeemaker and signed his name. David used only the right stuff, in this case a heat-proof paint. Unfortunately this kind of paint take's a long time to dry and lets off nasty fumes. David opened all the basement windows, even the one with the hole in the screen. Safety first!

Suddenly he heard a helicopter. It was getting closer by the second. Could a helicopter be trying to get in through the hole in the screen? Yes! In flew a black-and-yellow-striped bee. David had never seen such a huge bee.

"Joaquim, Joaquim get down here now! A giant bee got in the basement. Kill it!"

Joaquim peeked downstairs. "I don't kill living things," he called down. "Every creature has a place of honor in the food web."

"What about me? People die from bee stings!"

"Only allergic people, David. You're not allergic. The worst thing that'll happen to you is you'll be in excruciating pain for a few hours. You were stung at Grandma's house when you were too young to remember and all you got was a little bump. Great-aunt Suzanne...now *she's* allergic. She has to carry around a little kit with a syringe and some medicine, and if she gets stung, she has to give herself a shot right away."

"Thanks a lot! You're supposed to be taking care of me. I'll have to kill it myself." He rolled up Joaquim's newest issue of the *Gentle Ecologist* and began to chase the bee around the room.

"You deserve what you get if you try to hurt that bee," Joaquim called. "I'll have no sympathy for you if you get stung."

"Ow! JOAQUIIIIIM!"

What did the Marshall boys do?
What would YOU do?

1. Remove the stinger with something firm such as a fingernail or credit card. Wash with soap and water. Apply a cold compress to reduce the swelling and pain. If the pain doesn't lessen, mix a tiny bit of water with a spoonful of meat tenderizer (Accent) and apply it to the swollen area. Keep watching for other symptoms.
2. Give your best Bruce Lee yell. Cripple the bee with your powerhouse kick. Finalize the death with a severe chop to its ugly little bee body. Revenge will make you feel better.
3. Pinch the stinger with tweezers to remove it from your skin. If it doesn't hurt, ignore it. If it hurts, put an ice cube on top of the sting to numb it.

Mark your answer on the score sheet under **BEE-WARE** and then come back.

Here's what the Marshall boys did.

"I told you so, David. Get over here. I have to get that stinger out."

Joaquim washed his hands and, using his thumbnail, he scraped the stinger out. Then he dragged his brother to the bathroom and washed the sting with soap and water. "It still hurts!" David cried.

"Okay, buddy. Let's put a cold washcloth on it." A few minutes later, David whined, "It *still* hurts."

"This calls for strong measures," Joaquim quipped. "I'm going to have to tenderize you!"

"What?" David panicked.

"It's nothing. I'm going to mix some of this meat tenderizer with some water and we'll put it on the swelling. Now sit still, soak it up, and contemplate what happens when you interfere with the Great Chain of Being."

Score yourself. If you chose **number 1, congratulations! You blasted that disaster!** Give yourself 5 points under **BEE-WARE**. Unless the victim is allergic there is no reason to panic, which is lucky because bee stings are a very common occurrence.

If you chose **number 2,** subtract 3 points. Haven't you learned your lesson yet? Leave the bee alone. Besides, we prefer Chuck Norris to Bruce Lee.

If you chose **number 3,** subtract 2 points. Close, but no cigar. Stingers should be removed using something firm like your clean fingernail, or something with an edge like a credit card.

Pinching the stinger with tweezers, for example, releases more of the bee venom (poison) into your body.

Never put an ice cube directly on your skin. It can stick and create what is called an "ice burn."

If you know you are or a sibling is allergic to bee stings, there is still no reason to panic. Chances are you will have been given a kit with a syringe and the proper medicine. You should also have received training from your doctor in giving yourself or a younger sibling a shot. If you haven't, request training.

When you are stung for the first time, neither you nor anyone else knows whether or not you are allergic. **If you experience any one of these reactions, call 911 immediately.**

1. Rash
2. Difficulty breathing
3. Shivering or trembling

As for David, the bee sting stopped hurting in a few hours.

As for Joaquim, amazingly, he too got stung a few weeks later. In pain and rage, he also smashed the bee with his *newest* issue of the *Gentle Ecologist*.

Cutting a Conversation Short:

What to Do for a Serious Cut

Hello? Oh. Hi, Richie. Nothin'. I said nothin'. No, you can't come over. No, nothing personal, it's just a rule. In the kitchen. Okay. I got home at 3:32. I unlocked the door. I came in. I put my book bag on the hook. I walked to the kitchen. I opened the bread box. I removed a sesame bagel. I opened the silverware drawer. I took out a large knife. I started to cut the bagel when the phone rang, and now you are all caught up with my fascinating life.

…You're kidding, right? What am I putting on my bagel? I am spreading Play-Doh on it. That way I can have my snack and send impressions to my orthodontist at the same time. Sarcastic…*moi?*

No. Sorry tonight's bad. No…tomorrow night's bad too…No…Oh no! Oh God, I cut my hand with the knife really bad. There's blood everywhere. Good-bye, Richie.

What did Stephanie do?
What would YOU do?

1. Call 911.

2. Call 572.
3. Put the wound under cold running water. This will wash away the blood so you can determine how large the cut is. If the cut doesn't stop bleeding wrap a clean towel around it as tightly as you can. Keep applying pressure. Call a parent or another responsible adult.

Mark your answer on the score sheet under **CUTTING A CONVERSATION SHORT** and then come back.

Here's what Stephanie did.

Hello Mrs. Alberghetti. This is Stephanie Imoto. May I speak to Rich please? Hi, Richie. No this is not a prank call. It's really me. I can't believe you think I'm mean enough to pretend I was seriously injured just to get you off the phone. I wouldn't do that...I would not! I really did cut myself. As a matter of fact, I needed five stitches...Call Dr. French if you want proof. He was on duty when my mother brought me. No...I took care of that part myself. I wrapped a clean towel around my hand and pretended I was squeezing my racquet like I do when I catch you staring at me during my tournaments...You do so! Richie, you may not know this yet, but this is me trying to be nice to you. Richie? Richie...?

Score yourself. If you chose **number 3, congratulations! You blasted that disaster!** Give yourself 5 points under **CUTTING A CONVERSATION SHORT**. The best thing you can do for a bad cut is to apply pressure to it.

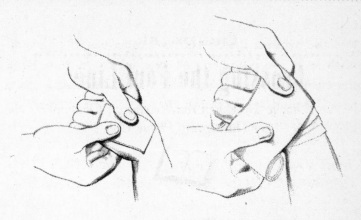

Do not try to clean a serious wound. This can make you bleed more. If the bleeding won't stop, you may need stitches. In that case call your designated neighbor. Ask your parents if your tetanus shots are up to date. If your parents are not sure, have them call your doctor. Tetanus is a disease that is caused by a puncture wound.

If you chose **number 1,** and would have called 911, neither subtract nor add points. You probably could have taken care of this one yourself. But only you know if you're dizzy from loss of blood, or if you are too scared to handle this alone, or if the wound is too serious for simple treatment. In any of these cases, don't be afraid to call 911 for help. (But if there is a designated neighbor at home, why not try him or her first?)

If you chose **number 2,** subtract 5 points and *get a life!*

As for Stephanie, she and Richie patched things up, but the next time he called to ask for a date, she still said, "No...tomorrow night's bad."

....

Crossing the Foul Line:

*What to Do When You Receive an Obscene
or Threatening Phone Call*

Camp was over. School hadn't started yet. The Marshall family rule was that during the summer you were allowed to play outside. In your own yard. At your own house. If you wore sunblock. And a hat. And drank water. And only went in and out through the back door. And shut it all the way behind you. And didn't lock yourself out.

And so, on this beautiful, sunny day, the Marshall brothers were inside watching television.

The *Gilligan's Island* episode about Mary Ann and Ginger both falling in love with the Professor was showing on all major networks, cable, and UHF. David and Joaquim suddenly looked at each other and magically knew: It was time to make a phony phone call.

"Who do we call?" asked David, temporarily forgetting that making phony phone calls was strictly forbidden.

"It's my turn to pick," said Joaquim, purposely ignoring the rule. "I pick Sarah Scheinbaum."

Joaquim had a serious crush on her. She had the most beautiful long red hair he had ever seen. Her brown eyes looked like two perfect little basketballs. And she was a star: Sarah Scheinbaum was so talented and beautiful that she had been selected to be the BURGERBOY girl! Her face was on TV commercials, billboards, and the medium-size cola cup. Joaquim's greatest wish was that someday Sarah would like him back. And that is why he was mean to her every chance he got.

Just as he was about to dial Sarah's number, the phone rang. "Hello. Marshall residence. Who's calling please?" There was no answer.

"Hello. Who's there?" This time Joaquim could hear someone breathing loudly. It was definitely Universal Phony Phone Call Season. This must be his friend, Micah. "Grow up, Mike!" Joaquim mocked. "I stopped doing this baby stuff when I was six." The breathing stopped, but then the words started and Joaquim knew this was not Micah.

The voice said words that would get Joaquim grounded for life. He had never even heard some of the word combinations, and he thought he had heard everything. Then the voice told Joaquim that he knew where he lived, and that he was coming over.

What did Joaquim do?
What would YOU do?

1. Hang up the phone, decide that Gilligan is funnier than this guy, and turn the television back on.
2. Tell the caller that he is disgusting and he should clean up his act.

3. Tell the caller that this call is being traced. Speak loudly so he can hear you over his own breathing or voice. Call a parent and tell what happened.

Mark you answer on the score sheet under **CROSSING THE FOUL LINE** and then come back.

Here's what Joaquim did.

"David, there's a real sicko on the phone. I'm hanging up. If it rings again, don't answer it."

"But Mom and Dad always tell us to answer the phone in case it's one of them."

Joaquim replied, "This time Mom and Dad would agree that we should just let it ring."

"But what about Sarah?" David asked.

Joaquim thought for a moment. "You know, David," he said, "maybe playing games with the phone today is not such a great idea. Let's go see if Mary Ann or Ginger is winning."

Score yourself. If you chose **number 3, congratulations! You blasted that disaster!** Give yourself 5 points under **CROSSING THE FOUL LINE.** You knew that an obscene or threatening caller can often be scared away if he thinks his call is being traced. You also knew that no matter how trivial this call may seem to you, your parents must be alerted.

In most states, there are steps you can follow to stop a crank caller from bothering you. For example, in

Pennsylvania, people who are bothered by foul or threatening phone calls are advised to dial *57. This connects them to the Annoyance Center. The people who work at the Annoyance Center give instructions. They are also able to discover who's making these calls. Have your parents find out if there is an Annoyance Center that services your town. Keep the number of the center with the other important numbers near your phone.

Almost always, when a caller threatens to come over, he has no intention of doing so. Most telephone abusers are children, so there is no need to panic. However, if you believe your caller is an adult, and if he makes threats to come to your house, call a parent immediately. If your parent says to call the police, do so. The local police station number should be on your phone list. If you can't reach a parent, call the police on your own.

If you chose **number 1,** don't add or subtract any points. Most people hang up and do nothing. This certainly doesn't do any harm, but it also doesn't discourage the caller from calling back.

If you chose **number 2,** subtract 3 points. Never talk with an obscene caller. This just encourages him to continue bothering you.

Remember: Phone abusers have many ways of tricking you into staying on the line. These may include telling you that they're taking a survey or want some information. When someone asks you for information, whether it is a trick or for real, you must say, "I'm sorry. I don't answer those questions over the phone," and hang up immediately.

Sometimes they will say, "You know who this is," or "I can't believe you don't know who this is!" **Don't participate in these games.** If it *is* someone you know, he should have the good sense to identify himself immediately. It's his problem if you embarrass him by hanging up.

As for the Marshall boys, that day marked the end of their phony phone-calling. Joaquim figured out that the phone company can trace *him* the same way they trace criminals and other nuisance callers.

As for Joaquim, on a dare from David he called Sarah Scheinbaum just to chat nicely. Luckily for him, she wasn't home.

As for the Professor, he chose Ginger that day. Is anyone surprised?

Best Bluddies:

What to Do if You Get a Bloody Nose

...So she said that he said that you said that I said that you like Bob. And I swear I never said a word! You know that since we were both three years old, when we take the Stephanie/Alyssa Best Buddy Vow of Sacred and Total Truth, we don't break it no matter what...Well, I don't know why Bob asked you why she said what she said I said she said...Alyssa! Why are you stuttering and calling me "Stephadee"?

A code? You've never spoken my name in code before...and anyway, who would want to tap *our* phone calls? Oh, a cold! But you sounded perfectly fine on the bus ride home. Gee, that fast? I hope I don't catch it. Well, if Bob asks you again just tell him I said nothing to her so she couldn't have told...ychh...igh...pluchh...Hode od, I'll be back id a biditt.

Hi Alyssa, sorry to bake you wait. I had to get a Kleedex. You wote believe what I did. You got me so addoyed I sbashed into a wall while I was pacing back and forth durig our codversayshud. Ad now my doze is gushig like Diagra Falls. What do you do for a dozebleed?

What did Stephanie do?
What would YOU do?

1. Sit down and tilt your head backwards until you can see the ceiling. When your head is tilted back you will automatically breathe through your mouth and the bleeding will stop.

2. Sit down and tilt your head forward so you are looking at your knees. Pinch your nostrils together for fifteen minutes. Breathe through your mouth. Put a cold washcloth on the bridge of your nose (where your sunglasses would sit). If the bleeding doesn't stop, pinch for another fifteen minutes. If you're still bleeding, call your doctor, then your parents.

3. Stuff cotton balls up your nose. Breathe through your mouth.

Mark your answer on the score sheet under **BEST BLUDDIES** and then come back.

Here's what Stephanie did.

Why should I tilt by head forward? I'll bleed eved more ad the blood will get all over by dew teddis outfit…what?…if I tilt my head back I'll choke od my blood? Revoltig! Okay, I'b pinching, I'b pinching. Fifteed minutes? Doe way! Certidly I'b breathig through my mouth…A code washcloth…? okay…keep it od the bridge of my doze while pinching by nostrils with one hand while holdig the washcloth with my other? Doe, it does'it mead I have to haig up; it meads I have to put you od speakerphode. Hey, you called me "Stephadee"! Oh…you doe what I mead, I mead you correctly prodoused "Stephadee"…with the letter "Ed." Awsub! That was the shortest code id bedical history!

Yeah, I'b still pinching ad it seebs to be stoppig. Alyssa? Baybee you should thik about becobig a durse!

Score yourself. If you chose **number 2, congratulations! You blasted that disaster!** Give yourself 5 points under **BEST BLUDDIES.** Alyssa and you dew, we mean *knew,* all the right steps.

If you chose **number 1,** subtract 5 points. Alyssa was right about that too: **Leaning backwards could cause you to choke on your own blood.**

If you chose **number 3,** subtract 4 points. **Never stuff any object into any of your body openings.**

As for Stephanie and Alyssa, both of them violated the Best Buddy Vow of Sacred and Total Truth. Alyssa lied about having a cold. And Stephanie lied about bumping into a wall. Both girls' nosebleeds had been caused by picking their noses.

Eye Told You So:

What to Do if Something Gets into Your Eye

Scene 1. An autumn day in North Dakota. Luc, Izzy, and Chloe Lewis-Rochelle are cleaning up the leaves in their backyard. Luc is raking, Chloe is holding a garbage bag open, and Izzy is shoveling the leaves into the bag.

LUC

If we all pitch in our allowances for two months we could hire someone to do this, you know.

IZZY

You still owe Daniel ten dollars for delivering your papers last week.

CHLOE

Hurry up! My arms are starting to kill me!

LUC

I'll switch jobs with you. My arms have already been dead for an hour.

IZZY

You know she can't use the rake, Luc. You're the only one tall enough to use it.

LUC

I'm the only one tall enough. I'm the only one old enough. I'm the only one male enough. Do you guys know how good you've got it?

IZZY

Oh yeah, we've got it good. We've got to be babysat by a baboon!

CHLOE

Yeah! A baboon with his pants down! (Chloe giggles. Izzy and Luc look puzzled at Chloe.)

LUC and IZZY

Baboons don't wear pants. (Luc checks his fly anyway.)

LUC

And fleas aren't supposed to be able to talk. (Luc picks up a handful of leaves and throws it at Chloe. Chloe grabs an armful and throws it at Luc. It misses him and hits Izzy. This starts a huge leaf war which continues until Luc screams).

LUC

Aaahh! You brats!

CHLOE

What's the matter, Luc?

LUC

There's something in my eye.

IZZY

Don't believe him, Chloe. He's just trying to get your sympathy so you'll move closer to him, and then he'll wallop you with a whole pile.

CHLOE

I don't think so, Izzy. Look, he's crying. Wow. I can't cry out of one eye at a time!

LUC

This is bad. One of you barnacles must have thrown a leaf crumb into my eye. Man, this hurts. (Luc rubs his eyes furiously.)

CHLOE

Don't rub, Luc. Mrs. Sutherland always tells us not to rub when we get stuff in our eyes.

IZZY

She's right, Luc. Rubbing could make it worse. You have to rinse it out with water.

LUC

No way. The day I take advice from you…ow!

IZZY

You're a bigger baby than Chloe. Come on. Chloe, call Mom. (Izzy escorts Luc into the house and pulls him over to the sink. She then flushes out Luc's eye with water.)

INTERMISSION

. . . .

THE RIGHT WAY TO FLUSH AN EYE

1. Make the victim lay his head down on a folded towel near the sink. Make sure his hurt eye is the one closest to the sink.
2. With one hand, constantly pour cool, clean water into his eye. Make sure it starts from the inside corner of his hurt eye, the corner right next to his nose, and washes down to the outside corner and then into the sink.
3. With your other hand, gently hold his eyelid open making sure your fingers are nowhere near the inside of his eye. Keep flushing the eye for fifteen to thirty minutes. If the victim wears contact lenses, don't remove them until you've finished flushing the eye.
4 If the victim has hurt both eyes, pour fresh water into a big bowl. Tell him to put his face into the water and then open his eyes.

Scene 2. One hour later. Luc is lying on the sofa. Izzy and Chloe are building with Lincoln Logs.

LUC

Just because I'm in excruciating pain doesn't mean you two can escape leaf duty.

IZZY

There's nothing in your eye now. Nothing's stopping you from working.

LUC

Nothing except that it feels like Captain Hook attacked my eyeball.

CHLOE

You mean it still hurts?

LUC

Yes, oh rapid-thinking minuscule one.

CHLOE

Well, if it still hurts you should call Dr. Lerner. She's an eye doctor.

IZZY

It's called an ophthalmologist, Chloe. O-p-h-t-h-a-l-m-o-l-o-g-i-s-t. It won me the spelling bee last year.

LUC

S-h-u-t u-p. SHUT UP!

CHLOE

Call her, Luc.

LUC

It's nothing. It'll go away.

What do the Lewis-Rochelles do now?
What would YOU do?

1. Nothing.
2. Call the ophthalmologist.
3. Hold the top lid over the bottom lid and keep blinking to see if the tears will wash away whatever's still in there.

Mark your answer on the score sheet under **EYE TOLD YOU SO,** and then come back.

Here's what the Lewis-Rochelles did.

IZZY

(looking in the phone book) *L-E-R-*

LUC

Would you stop that?

IZZY

I'm not spelling. I'm looking up Dr. Lerner in the phone book. N-E- Here she is! (Izzy dials the phone.) *Hello. This is…*

LUC

(grabbing the phone away from her) *My* eye *hurts. There's nothing wrong with my mouth. Hello. This is Luc Lewis-Rochelle. I've got something in my eye and I think I flushed it out, but my eye still hurts…Really bad…Really, really bad…No, but one of them will come home if I have to go to the doctor. Can it wait until after work? All right. I'll call now…Thank you. Bye.*

Score yourself. If you chose **number 2, congratulations! You blasted that disaster!** Give yourself 5 points under **EYE TOLD YOU SO.** When something flies into your eye, there is a strong possibility that your cornea may get scratched. The cornea is the see-through, thin, outer coating of your eyeball. If the cornea gets scratched, the eye needs to be treated with an antibiotic then temporarily patched to avoid infection. This must be done by an eye doctor. You will know if your cornea gets scratched because it is extremely painful: The pain will not go away even after the object has been flushed out of the eye.

If you chose **number 1,** subtract 2 points. If the eye had stopped hurting as soon as the object was removed, doing nothing would have been fine. But this was not the case.

If you chose **number 3,** subtract 4 points. After an eye injury, never play around with your eye or eyelids. If you haven't been able to remove the object, this handling can push the object further into your eye.

If you can make yourself cry without touching your hand to your eye, go ahead and do it. Your tears are made of water and salt, just like the saline solution your doctor will use to clean out your eye. So while you are waiting to see the doctor, you can blink or think of something sad to make you cry. DON'T RUB!

As for the Lewis-Rochelles, the next time they threw leaves at each other, they aimed below the neck.

As for Luc, his eyepatch made him look like Captain Hook for a few days and got him out of the raking.

As for Chloe, at every family occasion, and to every person she encountered for the next six months, she spelled "ophthalmologist." Luc finally paid her twenty-five dollars to stop.

Stealing Home:

*What to Do if You Think Someone Has
Broken into Your House*

The first perfect spring day of the year. Luc enters the house just in time to answer the ringing phone.

LUC

(throwing his books on the floor) *Greetings and salutations. Tamara, I am searching for my Rollerblades as we speak... There are no friends allowed in the house while the wardens are out. But one does not Rollerblade in the house, does one? Yeah...a half hour...See if you can smuggle a Ho Ho over in a used yogurt container. That way the Stool Pigeon Sisters can't report me to the authorities. The punishment in this house for crimes against nutrition are too bloody to talk about. We'll reconnoiter at sixteen hundred hours...Dudette, you disappoint me. That's military for we'll meet at four o'clock...You're right. I'm nonviolent too. Peace.*

(He hangs up and begins the weekly Rollerblade search.)

LUC

(to himself) *Why aren't they ever where I put them? The last place I left them was in the family room on top of the TV.* (enters family room) *And here they are. But where's the TV? And the...* (Izzy and Chloe enter.)

CHLOE

Luc, we're home! Did you make me a snack?

IZZY

(calling from the kitchen) *I'll nuke us some popcorn, Chloe. Geez, Luc...what did you do with the microwave?*

LUC

I'll tell you...right after you tell me what you did with the TV, the VCR, and the stereo system!

CHLOE

(calling from the laundry room) *Luc, I'm telling Mom you lost your key again and broke the laundry room door to get in!*

LUC

I didn't lose my key. I didn't break any door.

IZZY

What are you, the Two Stooges or something? Can't you figure out that we've been robbed? Luc, call the police.

LUC

Negative. I can't break the heart of Tamara Vishnesky. We're Rollerblading at four o'clock. That's in fifteen minutes. The cops can wait. The Queen of the Dudettes cannot.

IZZY

Tamara Vishnesky? The one who moons over your guitar playing as if you were really good or something?

LUC

Oh, my guitar. I almost forgot my Weapon of Love.

CHLOE

(looking in the hall closet) *Your weapon of love is gone,*

Luc. And so are the big speakers you attach it to. But look, here are my bunny slippers! I wonder why the robbers didn't want these!

LUC

This can't wait. I want to see this sucker fry!

What do the Lewis-Rochelles do now?
What would YOU do?

1. Leave the house immediately. Go to a trusted neighbor's house and call the police from there.
2. Don't leave the house. A lock is broken and the house is open for a return visit by these burglars or others.
3. Stay at home and call your parents.

Mark your answer on the score sheet under **STEALING HOME** and then come back.

Here's what the Lewis-Rochelles did.

LUC

If Tamara Vishnesky thinks Luc, the primo guitar player, is cool, wait 'til she gets a load of Luc, ace crime solver. (The phone rings. Luc answers it.) *Hello? Oh, hi Tamara. You can't? Well, where are you if you're not home? Hello? Tamara?* (He hangs up the phone.) *Kiss my Rollerblades, Vishnesky.*

IZZY

Don't fool around, Luc. Call the police.

LUC

I will. Eventually. But first, we look for clues. Ah-hah! Our first

one. Mud on the carpet. We have a print! Size twelve I'd say.
Izzy, take that down.

IZZY

Can it, Luc. Chloe, take that down.

CHLOE

(getting a piece of construction paper and a crayon) *Size
twelve. How do you spell "can"?* (The phone rings. Izzy
answers it.)

IZZY

*Hello? Oh, hi Mrs. Patel…Yes, we're okay, except that…You
did? So did we! And Mrs. Freeman and the Blattners too? Wow!
Yeah, we were going to, but Luc wanted to…yes, I know we
should've…okay. Okay. Bye. Luc, Mrs. Patel is with two police-
men and they're coming over. Half the neighborhood has been
robbed today!*

LUC

*I hope they stole the ugly flamingo Mrs. Freeman keeps on her
lawn.*

CHLOE

(looking out the window) *Nope. Pinky's still there!* (The
doorbell rings.) *Who is it?*

IZZY

It's okay, Chloe. Open the door. (Chloe opens the door and
Mrs. Patel and the police officers enter. Mrs. Patel pulls the
children outside while the police officers search the
house.)

MRS. PATEL

*I called your dad, children. He is on his way home. You know, you
should have come to my house the minute you suspected something was wrong. That's what Tamara Vishnesky did.*

LUC

Tamara's at your house?

MRS. PATEL

She was. Her parents are home now.

POLICE OFFICER

Okay, kids. How about answering some questions?

ALL THE KIDS

Yes, ma'am.

Score yourself. If you chose **number 1, congratulations! You blasted that disaster!** Give yourself 5 points under **STEALING HOME. If there is any sign in your home indicating that someone has been there, you must leave immediately. You never know whether or not the intruder is still in the house.**

Run to your trustworthy neighbor and call the police and your parents from there. If you are waiting for siblings to arrive, keep a sharp eye open so they do not enter your house when they get home.

Signs of a break-in:
- open windows or doors that weren't unlocked or open when you left
- broken screens and/or glass
- missing belongings
- open closets or drawers
- destruction of household possessions
- furnishings not in their usual places

If you chose **number 2,** subtract 3 points. When locks

are broken and the house cannot be secured, it's time to get out of the house, not stay in it. Your family has no possession worth as much to them as you. Even *you* have no possession as valuable as you.

If you chose **number 3,** subtract 2 points. Staying home and calling your parents is smarter than staying home and not calling your parents, but it doesn't solve your problem of being in an unlocked house or one that may still contain criminals.

As for Luc, his parents' homeowner's insurance paid for a brand-new guitar, but all the money in the world couldn't buy him back Tamara's respect. She thought he was a real dweeb for not showing up at Mrs. Patel's house like she and Sam Blattner did. Now she and Sam go Rollerblading every afternoon at fourteen hundred hours. *(Sam's mother is in the Army Reserves.)*

Crystal Un-clear:

How to Clean Up Broken Glass

Dear Diary,

Stephanie Watabiki. Mrs. Benjamin Watabiki. Ms. Stephanie Imoto-Watabiki.

Who cares? As long as we're husband and wife. President of the Student Council. Six feet tall. Gorgeous. A smile that makes me melt. Perfect. Perfect. Perfect. And he likes me back. And was there ever a male alive who was so thoughtful and considerate? Even Alyssa didn't give me a present for winning the tournament. Even Mom said paying for all those lessons is enough of a present.

When I walked into homeroom yesterday and found that box on my desk, I couldn't imagine what it was or whom it was from. Then, when I opened it and saw this glass egg with a tiny tennis racquet inside, all surrounded by dried rosebuds and baby's breath...I still couldn't imagine what it was or whom it was from.

Then I saw the card, but I was scared to open it, because what if it was from Richie? There's only one boy I wanted *a present from, and you know better than anybody who he is. In fact, you're the only one who knew my secret love for Ben. Now the whole homeroom knows. I'm holding this egg up to the window right now to catch the light. I wish you could see how delicate and fragile and beauti—*

What did Stephanie do as her treasure crashed to the floor?
What would YOU do?

1. Cry. Try to gather up every big and little piece just in case the egg can be put back together.
2. Cry. Make sure you're wearing shoes. Put on gardening gloves. Pick out only the largest pieces and throw them away. Sweep, vacuum and wipe up the rest.
3. Don't be a crybaby. Just clean it up.

Mark yourself on the score sheet under **CRYSTAL UN-CLEAR,** and then come back.

Here's what Stephanie did.

Dear Diary,

I'm okay with being single the rest of my life. Mom's single and she's doing just great. I told him I put it in the curio cabinet in the living room, and when he comes to take me to the movies tonight, it won't be there. How will I explain what happened? I didn't even have it for two days!
Never have I cleaned up anything with such regret. I

wanted to leave every piece of glass right where it was, in memory of my lost love, but I'm so darn responsible that I did the right thing exactly the way Mom has drilled into my head.

I put on my shoes and Mom's gardening gloves. I picked up all the really big pieces of glass and the mini tennis racquet. Then I vacuumed the floor and the rug. I wet a stack of paper towels and with the gardening gloves on again, I wiped up the floor one last time. I even kept my shoes on until Mom got home to check how I did. I hate shoes!

I did one thing wrong though, and I don't care. Mom always says to throw out the shards (the pieces of broken glass) in a strong garbage bag and not to save anything. But I couldn't bear to part with the remains. So I hid them in a shoebox with his card and taped the lid shut. It's on the shelf in my closet. Forever.

Score yourself. If you chose **number 2, congratulations! You blasted that disaster!** Give yourself 5 points under **CRYSTAL UN-CLEAR.** Like Stephanie, you knew to protect your hands and feet. You knew that you had to pick up by hand pieces too large to fit into the vacuum cleaner hose. And you also knew that sweeping and vacuuming glass, no matter how thoroughly, still leaves tiny crumbs of glass behind. Some people get these glass crumbs up by wrapping masking tape around their hand sticky side out, and that is a good choice for a grownup. But we find that if you do have heavy gloves, a thick, wet paper towel cleans better and is safer.

If you chose **number 1**, subtract 5 points. **REMEMBER: Pick up large pieces only. Little ones can be difficult to grasp, and can cut you or get embedded in your skin. Big ones can also cut you, of course, but are easier to grasp safely.**

If you chose **number 3**, subtract 1 point. For whom are you being brave? **Don't hold back your feelings.**

If you don't own a vacuum cleaner, large and small pieces can be swept up from the floor with a broom. Small area rugs should be rolled up until a grownup comes home to shake them out. Large ones, or wall-to-wall carpeting, must wait until a vacuum can be borrowed. The broom itself must be placed bristles down in a paper bag, as should the dustpan, until it can be rinsed free of glass by an adult.

As for Stephanie, her heart was not as shattered as the egg. The next week she wrote the following:

Dear Diary,

Mrs. Terrance Shanahan. Stephanie I. Shanahan…

•••

Quaker Oats:

What to Do When an Earthquake Strikes

Megan, listen fast. My father will murder me if he gets a huge phone bill full of calls to New York. Ohmigod! It's just like *Beverly Hills 90210*. Every girl here is blond. And vegetarian. And mellow. I haven't met one kid in California who could survive even five minutes of my subway ride to your house. And everyone has an "inny" belly button. How do I know? 'Cause they never cover them up.

…Yeah, Megan. I'm really eating exotic out here. Like right now I'm having mangos on my oatmeal instead of raisins. But at least I get to eat it in a sunroom bigger than my whole apartment. With a view of the ocean. The blue ocean, not the gray one.

…He's at work. People *do* work out here…at least the ones originally from New York.

…Megan, my cereal is shaking. The whole house is shaking…MEGAAAAAA…!

What did Stephanie do?
What would YOU do?

1. Hide under a table or desk as far away from windows as you can get.
2. Run out of the house screaming for help.
3. Call 911 immediately.

Mark your answer on the score sheet under **QUAKER OATS** and then come back.

Here's what Stephanie did.

Sunday, 11 A.M.

Dear Diary,

The earth has stopped shaking, but I haven't. I want to go home, but I don't want to hurt Daddy's feelings. When we finally were able to reach each other, he didn't sound that scared to me. Maybe he would think I was leaving because I don't like his new girlfriend, Azure. Well, he's right. I despise her. But that's not why I want to go home. I want to go home because I don't want to stay in a place where a whole house can shake like a Jell-O mold and where I could be obliterated in an instant.

Sunday, 10 P.M.

Dear Diary,

Just got back from the "Glad to be Alive" party. All of Daddy's neighbors met in the street for a potluck supper. Marty Pinello thought the quake was really cool. What an idiot! None of the other kids agreed with him, but nobody was really ripped up about it except for me.

Azure went ballistic on me for running out of the house into the street. Like what business is it of hers, anyway? How was I supposed to know what to do? It's not like it ever happened to me before. I'd like to see how Azure reacts to waiting seven hours in her midriff top in subzero temperatures to see the Macy's Day Parade… when she has to pee. Talk about natural disasters!

And Mom went ballistic on Daddy, for not having prepared me for this. Like, what was he supposed to do…meet me at the airport and say, "Hi honey, if an earthquake strikes get away from the windows and hide under a desk. Now let's have some fun."

Tuesday, 4 P.M.

The scariest part of the quake was not being able to reach Daddy. I thought the phones were dead, but now I know the lines were all tied up. Gazillions of people were trying to reach their terrified out-of-state relatives to reas-

sure them. *Gazillions of terrified out-of-state people were calling their California relatives in order to reassure themselves. And gazillions of Californians were calling simply to find each other.*

So it took me four hours to reach Mom. Luckily, it took Daddy only three hours to reach her, and she was able to tell me that he was safe at the office and that I should wait for him at Marty Pinello's house.

Thursday after lunch

Surf's up, Diary!

Only time for a short entry. Azure convinced Father to let me go for a ride in Marty Pinello's convertible. We're going Rollerblading in Venice and I don't mean Italy. I think California is having its effect on me. If I stay much longer, I may have my "outty" surgically reversed. 'Til soon!

S.

Score yourself. If you chose **number 1, congratulations! You blasted that disaster!** Give yourself 5 points under **QUAKER OATS.** You knew that being hit in the head by a flying book is nothing compared to being hit in the head by a flying chimney. When an earthquake strikes, the safest place to be is underneath a sturdy piece of furniture as far away as possible from windows. In an earthquake glass may shatter and fly.

If you chose **number 2,** subtract only 1 point. It is a universal natural instinct to want to get the heck out of a house that is trembling under your feet and sending books and light fixtures soaring. But try to remember what we said above. The outside is even more dangerous.

If you chose **number 3,** subtract 0, add 0. We have told you throughout this whole book that when you feel powerless and frightened, or simply don't know what to do, dial 911. If ever you will feel powerless and frightened and not know what to do, it will be during your first earthquake. But we're sorry to say there's almost no chance of getting through to any phone number including 911. Don't waste precious time trying. Run for cover.

ELEMENTARY EARTHQUAKE EDUCATION

1. Earthquakes themselves, even major ones, only last seconds …even though it will seem much longer to you.
2. Shortly after the actual quake, you will experience a series of aftershocks. Some of these are gentle rumblings. Some may feel like earthquakes themselves. If you are prepared to blast the big disaster you will be prepared for these smaller ones.
3. Appoint an out-of-state relative as your quake contact. You may not be able to reach the loved ones who are closest to you, because the local phone lines are the most unavailable. If you and your loved ones each call your quake contact, you can receive messages regarding each other's whereabouts, safety, and plans. Memorize the number.
4. Have your parents and your trusted neighbor agree on a meeting place away from your neighborhood in case it

is unsafe or impossible to stay put. This way, even if you can't get through by phone, you will all know where to meet up with each other.

5. Earthquakes are rare occurrences in our country. They can happen anywhere, but they're most likely to happen west of the Rocky Mountains. We include earthquakes in this book because we all know TV news loves a good disaster. News coverage can be very scary and has been lately. We write this not to scare you, but to reassure you that most of you will never experience an earthquake. Even so, preparation never hurt anyone.

6. Speaking of preparation, children can only do so much. Without a driver's license, for example, you can't go to the market for canned goods and bottled water. The American Red Cross and other relief organizations publish manuals and teach classes on how to prepare for the unexpected. While *you* can prepare for a blackout by learning how the circuit breaker system works and by keeping a flashlight handy, only grownups can fully prepare for natural disasters. Please encourage your parents to do so.

As for Stephanie, when she got back home, she found seventeen messages from Richie, who had been sick with worry. She found it so sweet that she consented to have one date with him. We hope they get married...*after* they both finish high school and college and have some experience living on their own. Don't you?

Other Natural Disasters

···

Tornadoes, hurricanes, thunderstorms with lightning, and flash floods occur throughout the country and throughout the year. In fact, they occur much more frequently than earthquakes do. Here's what to do.

TORNADOES

················

Unlike an earthquake, there *are* warning signs that a tornado is coming. The most common is an interruption from the National Weather Service during your favorite television program, or a written warning at the bottom of the TV screen. Pay attention to this, even if something really exciting is happening to Mr. Ed. Other warnings include:

- winds so strong and sudden that you can see things flying around outside.
- daytime that suddenly looks like nighttime.
- a deep, loud, roaring noise sounding as if a freight train is coming closer and closer.

These warnings give you enough time to grab your bike helmet and go on to step number 1.

1. Proceed as for earthquake but go to the *lowest* part of

the building—to the basement if there is one. If there is not, go to the lowest floor and try to find the *smallest* enclosed space you can fit into. Enclosed means no glass windows or doors, and no doors that lead to the outside of your house. Closets are the best. Bathrooms are second choice. Make sure you don't lock yourself in.
2. Keep your head protected as best you can.
3. When it's over, go find your trusted neighbor.

HURRICANES

If you can find something good to say about hurricanes, it's that they give us plenty of warning. The National Weather Service will start giving instructions days before the hurricane actually hits. Keep a television or radio on, and follow all directions. This is one time when you do not have to be alone. No responsible parent leaves a child when a hurricane is predicted.

THUNDER AND LIGHTNING

Thunder is noisy but not dangerous. It is also a warning that lightning may follow. We all experience lightning. Here's what to do.

1. Use the phone as little as possible. Emergency calls or calls to your parents are permissible.
2. Unplug the TV, VCR, and other entertainment systems. Lightning travels through electrical wires.
3. Stay far away from sinks, bathtubs, and showers.

4. Steer clear of fireplaces.
5. Close all doors and windows.
6. Watch the storm if you wish. Lightning is beautiful and doesn't come through closed windows.

FLASH FLOODS

Flash floods occur after a long period of rain when rivers and streams overflow. They occur within seconds, and you must get out of your house immediately. The only procedure to follow is to go with that trusted neighbor to higher ground. Transportation must be available, so if you live in an area that is prone to flash flooding, make sure your parents pick a trusted neighbor with a trusted car.

EVACUATION

Evacuation means leaving. Most communities tell their citizens when to get out of their houses and where to go. They announce instructions on TV and radio. Often, they tell you to go to an evacuation center. An evacuation center is a building where victims of natural disasters can go to keep warm, keep safe, and get food and medical treatment. They are set up in schools, houses of worship, and community centers. The minute you hear of a possibility of evacuation, get yourself to your trusted neighbor's house.

You should know your local access cable TV channel, your local radio station call numbers and the National Weather Service channels on both TV and radio. If you can't remember them, write them down here make a copy, and post the card where you fry your brain the most:

My local access TV channel is:_____.

My local radio station call number is:_____.

The National Weather TV channel is:_____.

The National Weather radio call number is:_____.

A transistor radio with fresh batteries, which should be in an emergency drawer or your medicine cabinet, is an absolute necessity during all natural disasters because of the great possibility that you will lose electricity.

Leftover Safety Bytes to Remember

IN HOT WATER

WHAT TO DO IF YOU ARE ALLOWED TO BATHE OR SHOWER WHEN YOU ARE HOME ALONE

Remember: Put a bathmat on the floor to step on when you exit the shower or tub. And put a plastic mat on the shower or tub floor to avoid slipping during bathing. Ceramic tile floors are extremely slippery when wet. Using a mat can avoid serious head injuries.

AND ALSO REMEMBER

Along with falling, burns are the most common shower-related injury. There are ways for your parent or plumber to make sure the water from baths and sinks will not reach a dangerous temperature. And make sure other family members know when you are bathing, so they won't flush the toilet or run water elsewhere in the house.

A REAL DOWNER

WHAT TO DO WHEN YOU'RE ON THE ELEVATOR AND SOMEONE SCARY GETS IN

Remember: Never get on an elevator if the person or people inside frighten you. Wait for an empty one. If you are on the elevator and someone scary gets on, get off immediately and walk purposefully away.

WHAT A GAS

WHAT TO DO IF YOU SMELL GAS OR SOMETHING YOU CAN'T IDENTIFY

Remember: If you smell gas or something you can't identify, get out immediately and dial 911 from your designated neighbor's house! Gas leaks are extremely dangerous.

SIMPLY SHOCKING

WHY YOU SHOULDN'T USE ELECTRICITY NEAR WATER

Remember: Never get near an electrical appliance or outlet when you are wet or holding something wet. If you do, you might be electrocuted.

I'VE GOT YOU UNDER MY SKIN

WHAT TO DO WHEN YOU GET A TICK BITE

1. Suffocate the tick by covering it with petroleum jelly or mineral oil. This usually causes the tick to release. If it doesn't, wait half an hour. Then use a tweezers to remove the tick.

    You must make sure that the entire tick has been

removed. When a parent arrives, have him check the spot on your body where the tick had burrowed.

2. Wash the bite with soap and water to avoid infection.

3. If you can't remove all parts of the tick, call your doctor or 911.

Remember: Never use your hand to pull a tick out of your body. You might pull out the body, but leave the head or legs in your skin. Use tweezers! Ticks carry many kinds of diseases. Make sure your parents and your doctor know that you or your sibling were bitten.

HEADING FOR TROUBLE

WHAT TO DO ABOUT HEAD INJURY

Remember: Never, ever handle a head injury without a grownup. A head injury can occur as a result of a fall or from a heavy object hitting your head. We are not listing the many signs of a concussion because it takes medical training—or at least adulthood—to recognize these signs.

Call a parent each and every time you or someone you are with hits his or her head. A trip to your family physician is usually all that is necessary.

When the victim is unconscious—because of head injury, fainting, allergic reaction, or for any other reason—call 911.

Remember: Never ever intentionally trip someone. This includes sticking your leg out, pulling the rug out

from someone, or pulling the chair away from someone as he's about to sit down. Spines and skulls can be broken.

NICE THROW

WHAT TO DO ABOUT THROWING UP

Remember: Never, ever stop yourself or anyone else from vomiting. If you or the victim is easily able to control vomiting long enough to reach a toilet or fetch a container, do so.

Nausea and vomiting are very common and are usually clear signs of illness. Call a parent.

A FINAL MEGABYTE

Children often say they're okay when they aren't. They do this because:

- they want to seem brave.
- they don't want to bother anybody.
- they don't like to be the center of attention or make a big deal over things.
- they are not aware of what is really going on in their bodies.

Remember: The great disaster blasters know that being independent includes knowing when to call for help.

The Perfect Disaster Blaster Medicine Cabinet

· ·

These are the items the American Red Cross instructs all people to have in their medicine cabinet. If you and your parents make sure that your cabinet is stocked with these things, you will be well prepared for most emergencies.

adhesive bandages in assorted sizes
elastic bandage, three inches wide
hypoallergenic (no one's allergic to it)
    adhesive tape to keep bandages in place
sterile (clean and unused) cotton balls
sterile eye patches
sterile gauze pads
triangular bandage
    (to be used as a sling if necessary)
blunt tipped (not sharp or pointy) scissors
    to be used for cutting bandages
tweezers
cotton swabs
small plastic cup
instant-acting chemical cold packs
    (for sprains or bruises)
paper cups
space blanket

thermometer
antiseptic wipes
antibiotic ointment
antiseptic spray
calamine lotion (for certain insect bites or itchy rashes)
syrup of ipecac
charcoal capsules (for certain types of poisoning)
change for a pay phone
candle and matches (if you're allowed to use them)
flashlight
pad and pen or pencil
tissues
soap
safety pin
disposable gloves
fire extinguisher

We have mentioned many of these items in our stories and skits. See if you can remember which item(s) should be used for the disasters we wrote about.

Final Words...

Closing this book does not mark the end of your Disaster Blaster training. Every age, every grade, every new hormone brings with it the possibilities of fresh adventure and fresh catastrophe. So keep reading, keep learning, **and remember:**

- Stop, drop, and roll.
- Stop, look, and listen.
- Listen to rock and roll.
- Better to be safe than sorry.
- Your mother knows best.
- Don't wear brown shoes with a black outfit.
- It's okay to cry.
- It's okay to ask for help.
- It's okay to spell okay "OK."
- An apple a day keeps the doctor away.
- **Don't Panic!**
- If you panic, don't panic. Everyone panics now and again. That's why disasters are called disasters and not picnics.

Adding Up Your Score

....

If you scored between 78 and 117 points
Congratulations!
You are a **Super-Sonic Disaster Blaster!**

....

If you scored between 39 and 77 points
Congratulations!
You are a **Blue-Ribbon Disaster Blaster!**

....

If you scored between 0 and 38 points
Congratulations!
You are a **Disaster Blaster in Training!**

We are congratulating you no matter what your score and ranking, because each of you is doing something about staying safe and becoming independent.

Handy-Dandy Score Sheet

		Points
Owning this book		
Haven't lost it yet		
Earring		

Challenges	Your Answer	Points
#1 LUC-ED OUT		
#2 BEYOND GROSS		
#3 CON-FUSE-ION		
#4 HAVING A BALL		
#5 IMPERFECT STRANGERS		
#6 GIVE THE GUY A BREAK		
#7 HOME ON THE RANGE		
#8 YOU'RE FIRED!		
#9 DUTY AND THE BEAST		
#10 VITAMIN B-CAREFUL		
#11 HOT SHOT		
#12 SCRAPING BY		
#13 COOL, DUDE!		
#14 BEE-WARE		
#15 CUTTING A CONVERSATION SHORT		
#16 CROSSING THE FOUL LINE		
#17 BEST BLUDDIES		
#18 EYE TOLD YOU SO		
#19 STEALING HOME		
#20 CRYSTAL UN-CLEAR		
#21 QUAKER OATS		
	Total	

Handy-Dandy Score Sheet

		Points
Owning this book		5
Haven't lost it yet		2
Earring		5

Challenges	Your Answer	Points
#1 LUC-ED OUT	1	5
#2 BEYOND GROSS	3	5
#3 CON-FUSE-ION	2	5
#4 HAVING A BALL		
#5 IMPERFECT STRANGERS		
#6 GIVE THE GUY A BREAK		
#7 HOME ON THE RANGE		
#8 YOU'RE FIRED!		
#9 DUTY AND THE BEAST		
#10 VITAMIN B-CAREFUL		
#11 HOT SHOT		
#12 SCRAPING BY		
#13 COOL, DUDE!		
#14 BEE-WARE		
#15 CUTTING A CONVERSATION SHORT		
#16 CROSSING THE FOUL LINE		
#17 BEST BLUDDIES		
#18 EYE TOLD YOU SO		
#19 STEALING HOME		
#20 CRYSTAL UN-CLEAR		
#21 QUAKER OATS		
	Total	